THE WOMAN-CENTERED UNIVERSITY

Interdisciplinary Perspectives

Edited by

Melanie McCoy
JoAnn DiGeorgio-Lutz

University Press of America,® Inc.
Lanham • New York • Oxford

Copyright © 1999 by
University Press of America,® Inc.
4720 Boston Way
Lanham, Maryland 20706

12 Hid's Copse Rd.
Cumnor Hill, Oxford OX2 9JJ

Library of Congress Cataloging-in-Publication Data

The woman—centered university : interdisciplinary perspectives /
edited by Melanie McCoy, JoAnn DiGeorgio-Lutz.
p.   cm.
Includes bibliographical references.
1. Sex discrimination in higher education—United States. 2.
Women—Education (Higher)—United States 3. Educational
equalization—United States. I. McCoy, Melanie. II. DiGeorgio-
Lutz, JoAnn.
LC212.862.W66   1999 378'.0082—dc21   99—34905 CIP

ISBN 0-7618-1459-0 (cloth: alk. ppr.)
ISBN 0-7618-1460-4 (pbk: alk. ppr.)

For

Michael and Matthew

JDL

iii

Contents

Preface

The idea of writing this book grew out of the work of a small number of women faculty and administrators at Texas A&M University--Commerce. The women at TAMU-C who first developed the idea for the book decided to ask women on this campus and on other university campuses if they would like to contribute to a book on women in higher education. We asked that they address the central question "If a university was to commit itself fully to provide women an equal education, what would it need to do and what particular barriers exist that prevent change in this direction?"

We are not providing the reader with a blueprint on how to make the university woman-centered, nor do we believe we have answered the question in its entirety. We do hope that through our work we can demonstrate to the reader that those of us in the trenches can make a difference in our own universities. We also informed the prospective authors that the book's approach was to be interdisciplinary, multicultural, and applied. Subsequently, fifteen women and one male contributed to this book.

The chapters presented in this book have their inherent limitations. They represent only a small number of disciplines and even less policy related areas within the university system. We believe this limitation primarily reflects the tragic state of affairs regarding women in institutions of higher learning. However, as proponents of change, we believe that our insights and experiences presented in this work will contribute to the critical mass needed to generate awareness and action for the creation of a woman-centered university to the benefit of all women.

Acknowledgments

Many individuals contributed to the completion of this work. First and foremost we want to thank the Women's Association at Texas A&M University-Commerce for their immeasurable support. We especially want to thank those members of the Association, including Kenneth Miller, who contributed chapters to this book. Their fortitude under our occasional exacting demands over chapter deadlines and other pertinent information serves as a testament to the strength and power of women in higher education for whom this work was originally conceived. We would also like to thank those women who contributed chapters to this work whose academic locales extend beyond our East Texas frontiers. Their contributions acutely illustrate that the need to construct a woman-centered university transcends academic disciplines as well as geographic space. We would also like to extend a special thank you to Dana Phelps who helped build the index for this book.

A special thank you is in order for our families who bore the weight of our remonstrance over the past two years, especially as this book began to take its final form. Additionally, we would like to recognize and thank our students and women faculty everywhere. It is our hope that they and those who follow in their pursuit of higher education will benefit in some way from the prescriptions and insights that the contributors to this work intended. Lastly, we would like to thank our colleagues in the Department of Political Science, Paul Lenchner, Charles Elliott, and Charlie Embry, who are beginning to embrace the idea of change amidst a growing and unwavering matriarchy of two.

Introduction

Melanie McCoy and JoAnn DiGeorgio-Lutz

It often takes a critical mass to bring about institutional change. Even though change is never an easy process, there seems to be some magical number or combination of persons who must act to prod an institution out of its inertia. Moreover, for change to occur, there must be one or more persons within the institutional structures who act as catalysts for change, who motivate and mobilize others, and who attempt to create the support needed throughout the institution to achieve reform.[1] The institution that is the focus of this book is the university. Even with the civil rights and women's rights movements of the 1960s and 1970s, universities today remain fundamentally unchanged. The knowledge base is essentially the same and European-male educational norms remain as standards that persist in judging women and people of color. Women students, faculty, and administrators continue to accommodate themselves to study, teach, and engage in scholarship in the European-male tradition.[2] Schuster and Van Dyne use the term "invisible paradigms" to describe how education for and about men shapes higher education.[3] Even though women are numerically in the majority in higher education, they still find themselves treated as a minority group by a shrinking population of European-males who continue to dominate university goals and values. According to Pearson, et al. being the majority is a state of mind, a locus of power that defines, enforces and controls. Acting as the dominant group in U.S. society, European-males use the educational system to legitimize and retain their power on other grounds. The university is a powerful tool through which the dominant group can reinforce its cultural beliefs and define economic relationships that confer on them privileges as the ranking dominant group in society.[4]

According to Myra and David Sadker, 53 percent of all college students are women. Consequently, many people now perceive that the barriers to women in higher education no longer exist. However, the Sadkers believe that transparent and invisible walls have only replaced the more visible brick walls that still confront women and other minorities in educational settings. Men and women still are unequal in higher education. The Sadkers provide the following data to support their assertions: approximately 70 percent of students in the hard sciences (physics, chemistry, computer science) are male; institutions of higher learning award 85 percent of all bachelors degrees in engineering to men along with 69 percent of all degrees in agriculture and 61 percent of all architecture degrees. On the other side of the glass wall are the "soft" sciences and humanities where the majority of women earn 75 percent of the education degrees; 66 percent of psychology, communications, and performing arts degrees and 84 percent of health science degrees. Even though women are concentrated primarily in these disciplines, 56 percent of the "soft" sciences and humanities faculty are men. Women entering graduate school find the climate even more hostile than in undergraduate programs. Women earn half as many doctorates as men. Men still continue to earn 75 percent of the doctorates in business and 91 percent in engineering. Even when women earn their doctorates and enter academia, they face inequality. Sixty-eight percent of the male faculty has tenure compared to only 45 percent of female faculty members. Given this state of affairs regarding women and institutions of higher learning, we believe that the time is ripe to initiate institutional change.

The idea of writing this book grew out of the work of a small number of women faculty and administrators at Texas A&M University--Commerce. Three years ago a group of junior faculty women started the TAMU-C Women's Association, building on the work of a group that preceded it, the Council on Women's Issues. With minimal funding and an equally small membership, the Women's Association aimed it efforts at making the university more "woman-centered." The association traveled down the same road that many such groups have gone in the past. It held a women's symposium, started publishing a newsletter, opened an Office of

Women's Resources, celebrated "Women's History Month," and established a women's research support group.

The activity sponsored by the TAMU-C Women's Association that received the least notice may have the potential to bring about the most significant change in the institution--the women's research support group. Out of this group came the original idea for this book. A few of the women had begun to see that any changes we had made in the university to make it more woman-centered were at the margins. It was what Peggy McIntosh called the "add women and stir" approach.[5] For a university to be woman-centered there has to be a paradigm shift, a shift that substitutes a world view of inclusion in which the needs of males would be as important, but not more important, than that of majority females and minority males and females.[6] Gender matters. It is not enough for us to just accept differences in gender. One must also acknowledge and respect the differences among us. Not to notice differences is not to recognize that the university is excluding people of color and women from the curriculum, pedagogy, language, and other important aspects of a university education.[7]

The contributors to this book realized that to transform the university meant not only transforming the curriculum but also the faculty, the administrators, the teaching and learning process, and the university climate as a whole. A woman-centered university would require simultaneous attacks on multiple fronts to change the who, the what, and the how of the university. Why are there so few women faculty members, so few women chairs of departments and critical committees, so few women deans and so few women administrators? It is still possible for a woman to graduate from a co-educational school without ever studying with a tenured woman professor. Men comprise 68 percent of the faculty and of these 59 percent are European-males. Of the 32 percent of the faculty that are women, 28 percent of these are European-females. Moreover, as faculty ranks increase, one finds fewer women. Seventy-six percent of all full professors are men. People of color make up less than 12 percent of all faculty members and women of color are less than 5 percent of the faculty. Why is this important? We believe it is important because it means that undergraduate women and men have few, if any, strong female role models. Secondly, without a critical mass of women faculty and administrators in positions of power, significant change may not occur and a woman-centered university may not become a reality.[8]

The authors of *The Chilly Classroom Climate: A Guide to Improve the Education of Women* contend that if the curriculum and classroom are not transformed women will face a "chilly classroom climate". This term describes a subtle ambiance in which many small inequities create a negative atmosphere for learning, for teaching, and for fulfilling professional roles on campus. Mary Rowe used the term "micro-inequities" to describe the small, everyday interactions in classrooms and on campus in which individuals find themselves treated differently because of gender. These micro-inequities have a cumulative effect that creates unequal educational opportunities for women. It is not enough to integrate women into the curriculum, and that includes all women, not just white, middle-class women. If the university is truly to become woman-centered, then universities must also address the critical issues of how women are taught and how they are treated both in and out of the classroom.

To build a woman-centered university, faculty and administrators would have to consciously and deliberately commit themselves to meet the educational needs of all women. Equal access to higher education is not the same as equal educational opportunity. If women are disadvantaged by their gender then they do not receive an equal education comparable to men.[9] The central question we want to address in this book is, "If a university was to commit itself fully to provide women an equal education, what would it need to do and what particular barriers exist that prevent change in this direction?" One can infer that from the nature of the complex question posed that this book would have an applied, practical approach addressing the question's key topic. One could also infer that the book would need to be interdisciplinary in scope because women are part of virtually all university disciplines. Teaching women's studies courses or making a small number of changes in a few courses or disciplines does not substitute for the inclusion of women in the scholarship of all disciplines. Finally, if the university is truly to become woman-centered, then this book cannot limit itself exclusively to the needs of white, middle and upper class women. Many scholars engaged in much of the research on women in higher education have confined their work to white, middle and upper class women. This research often does not acknowledge the cultural and racial differences of women. In this book we acknowledge the interactions of gender, ethnicity, and other cultural "differences."

Introduction

The women at TAMU-C who first developed the idea for the book decided to ask women on this campus and on other university campuses if they would like to contribute to a book on women in higher education. We asked that they address the central question "If a university was to commit itself fully to provide women an equal education, what would it need to do and what particular barriers exist that prevent change in this direction?" We are not providing the reader with a blueprint on how to make the university woman-centered, nor do we believe we have answered the question in its entirety. We do hope that through our work we can demonstrate to the reader that those of us in the trenches can make a difference in our own universities. We also informed the prospective authors that the book's approach was to be interdisciplinary, multicultural, and applied. Subsequently, fifteen women and one male contributed to this book.

The chapters presented in this book have their inherent limitations. They represent only a small number of disciplines and even less policy related areas within the university system. We believe this limitation primarily reflects the tragic state of affairs regarding women in institutions of higher learning. However, as proponents of change, we believe that our insights and experiences presented in this work will contribute to the critical mass needed to generate awareness and action for the creation of a woman-centered university to the benefit of all women.

In chapter one, Kate Conway-Turner examines the academic culture that African-American female assistant professors encounter when they enter the university system. She also assesses the impact of race and gender as African-American professors maneuver the system and offers some strategies for overcoming the barriers to achieving tenure.

Juanita Firestone in chapter two sociologically assesses the level of job satisfaction between male and female faculty members within one university system. She discerns areas of difference in satisfaction according to gender and academic area including the impact of rank and tenure status and perceptions of glass ceilings.

In chapter three, Ken Miller, Susan Miller, and Gwen Schroth examine the dynamics of gender bias and discrimination in our nation's colleges and universities. Additionally, they offer a model to promote gender equity and justice as a step toward achieving a woman-centered university.

In chapter four, Donna Arlton, Ara Lewellen, and Barbara Grissett evaluate the psychological and social barriers that affect the promotion, rank, and salary structure of women faculty. Providing both an historical overview and current analysis of the situation, the authors then suggest ways in which universities can increase women's parity with their male counterparts through a social systems perspective.

Chapter five by JoAnn DiGeorgio-Lutz examines the shortcomings of the gender-biased foundations of International Relations as a field of Political Science. She offers a pedagogic approach based on collaborative learning techniques as a means to actively include women and other minorities in both the classroom environment and the IR curriculum.

In the field of anthropology, Helen Johnson in chapter six examines the ways in which the educational process intersects with potentialities for social change, particularly elucidating the connections between feminist politics and the role which education can play in the development of individuals with a commitment to social justice.

In the area of elementary education, Martha Foote and Carole Walker recognize that children's literature is a "powerful resource" for investigating gender-biased issues. In chapter seven they discuss the ways in which they identify the treatment of gender in children's literature and discuss the implications of this process when women begin to ask "hard questions" related to gender.

Margaret Madden discusses the paucity of representation of diverse women in the psychology curriculum in chapter eight. She also notes that when women are included, they tend to be compared with men or members of ethnic minority groups within the dominant Anglo culture. Moreover, Madden notes that when diversity is included, it often provokes defensiveness when viewed from the perspective that race may affect behavior rather than vice-versa.

Chapter nine, by Sharon Shelton-Colangelo and Lynn Becker Haber, demonstrates the positive aspects of collaborative learning as they discuss their unique experiences at writing a collaborative dissertation. They aptly illustrate that the transformation of the doctoral experience can contribute to the formation of a woman-centered university when women's ways of thinking, speaking, and knowing are consciously incorporated into the educational experience.

In the conclusion, we evaluate the preceding chapters to determine how closely we assessed the central question we assigned to all those who contributed to this book.

Notes

1. Pearson, Carol S., Donna L. Shavlik, and Judith G. Touchton. 1989. *Educating the Majority: Women Challenge Tradition in Higher Learning.* New York: Collier-Macmillan.

2. Pearson, et al., 7-8.

3. Schuster, Marilyn and Susan Van Dyne. 1984. "Placing Women in the Liberal Arts Curriculum". *Harvard Education Review,* (54): 413-428.

4. Jones, Terry and Gale Auletta Young. 1997. "Classroom Dynamics: Disclosing the Hidden Curriculum." In *Multicultural Course Transformation in Higher Education,* eds. Ann Intilli Morey and Margie K. Kitano. Boston: Allyn and Bacon.

5. McIntosh, Peggy. 1989. "Curricular Re-vision: The New Knowledge for a New Age." In *Educating the Majority: Women Challenge Tradition in Higher Learning,* eds., Carol S. Pearson, Donna L. Shavlik, and Judith G. Touchton. New York: Collier-Macmillan.

6. Pearson, et. al., 365.

7. Sandler, Myra and David Sadker. 1994. *Failing at Fairness: How Our Schools Cheat Girls.* New York: Simon and Schuster.

8. Sandler and Sadker, 29.

9. Diller, Ann, Barbara Houston, Kathryn P. Morgan, and Maryann Ayim. 1996. *The Gender Question in Education: Theory, Pedagogy, and Politics.* Boulder, CO: Westview.

Chapter 1

Maneuvering the Academic Culture: Insights and Strategies Within the Tenure Process

Kate Conway-Turner

African American women and other women have a rocky terrain to cross as they prepare to and successfully achieve tenure and the promotion that assures security within the academic arena. Newly appointed assistant professors often begin their position relieved to have managed the initial hurdle of entry, while neglecting to keep their eyes squarely upon the forthcoming tenure process. The neglect of this foresight can be disastrous and often this issue is brought to light only after the first academic review (typically occurring during the third year). The negative comments sometimes seen in this evaluation alarm many faculty members. They report that they have been working very hard, teaching heavy course loads, laboring on departmental, college and university committees, and pursuing research only to be told that they are lacking evidence of sufficient scholarship and that this trend is problematic for upcoming tenure. This chapter examines the academic culture that African American female assistant professors find when entering the academy. Further, I discuss the impact of race and gender on maneuvering this system, the importance of understanding the university structure and finally strategies that can be used to master the process and successfully gain tenure accompanied by an academic promotion.

University Culture

Universities have three broad goals that are typically stated within the mandate of all universities. These institutions seek to transmit information and culture to students, increase knowledge through research, and provide service to the university and broader community (Farley 1990). Although the priority of each goal varies somewhat depending on the type of institution (liberal arts college, research university or state university), each is seen as an important component. However, research in the form of publications has been documented as "the single most important factor in hiring, promoting and tenuring academics" (Phillips 1993). Thus although all goals are rhetorically seen as important, it is research publications that create the academic stamp of approval.

The academic culture permeates the entire university structure, however it is within a faculty member's department that most faculty members acutely experience the university culture as reflected within their specific discipline (Verrier 1992). The reality of what is seen as important, the process that is seen as legitimate and the rules and standards that faculty are judged by are seen most saliently within individual departments. All departmental cultures regardless of the present gender and racial composition, reflect a white male centered culture (Lie and O'Leary 1990; Welch 1990). This culture consists of an expectation that a white male model will be the standard to judge all candidates for tenure. This model consists of a strong and tightly focused research or scholarship agenda which culminates in a long line of scholarly publications within the top mainstream journals. It consists additionally of a record of teaching that varies widely between universities and both of these factors are accompanied by some evidence of service. The faculty member's record according to this model will be established within a 6 years time frame with little room for negotiation, flexibility in focus, individual differences or creativity. These criteria give very little if any acknowledgement to faculty members extensive work with undergraduate or graduate students or those faculty members who are deeply involved in service activities. Parker (1994) suggests that both teaching and service are devalued within the university's male centered environment. She further attests that work with students is seen as "childcare" and that the committee work necessary to keep the university community functioning is seen as "housework". Thus both are viewed as women's work which therefore merits no value within the university culture.

This androcentric and inflexible expectation underlying the judgment of the merit of a faculty member, suits some white male faculty, but not all and few people of color—particularly African American women. This model assumes a "person" (male) enters the academic arena, already with colleagues to collaborate with, funds for research and a life style that allows you to focus most, if not all of your time, establishing a research agenda and a national reputation. It assumes that teaching loads are equivalent within a department. Further, it does not make a difference between a faculty member who is given a lighter load because they have a research grant, nor does it take into account class size or number of new preparations. It also assumes that research is the only true way of distinguishing yourself with the academic community. The assumptions made fit best the role of a white male that enters a welcoming and familiar system who is either without a family or has a wife to shoulder all responsibilities until after he has received the security of tenure. This model fits few faculty members in the 1990's, but most certainly disadvantages African American faculty. The present academic culture does not understand the inherent racism and sexism in its policies, nor are universities motivated to change the standards. The policies are inflexible and allow little room for unique contributions. Any assumption that the academic environment welcomes, supports or understands the needs of African American faculty is dangerously flawed.

African-American Women on University Campuses

African American faculty have the lowest progression and retention rate within the academy (Moses 1989; Johnsrud 1993; Clague 1992; Touchton and Davis 1991). Additionally data indicates that the majority of women and people of color are concentrated in less prestigious universities and that they are disproportionally found within the lower ranks (Olsen, Maple and Stage 1991; Bronstein, Rothblum and Solomon 1993).

Clague describing a Maryland University documented that of the fourteen African American faculty that were hired between 1982-85 only one remained in 1992, thus representing a loss of 93 percent of the faculty entering in those years. It is also well documented that many women and African Americans leave the institution before going up for tenure, counter to the assumption that they leave after being denied tenure. Thus there are critical turning points in the career of African American women when a decision to stay or leave the academy is made (Boice 1993).

Associated with what might be called a critical turning point is the dissatisfaction that African American women feel in many academic environments. Research reveals that males are more likely to be "very" satisfied with the academic environments than females and whites are more satisfied than African Americans (Clague 1992). Thus African American women are more likely to experience dissatisfaction than other comparison groups.

The sources of dissatisfaction stem from what is perceived as racism or sexism within the academy. Many investigators have documented a long list of stressors related to the gender and race of African American women faculty (Boice 1993; Clague 1992; Fisher 1988; Phillip 1993; Welch 1990). Women commonly report experiencing isolation within their departments. Typically these feelings of isolation are connected with the perception that they are not welcome or respected within their departments. As one tenure track assistant professor stated, "I always feel like I need to protect myself, that every word I say is being reviewed to prove that I am something less than my white male peers". Thus her reaction is to isolate herself and to measure her words carefully and to not engage in unnecessary dialogue with her departmental colleagues. Others express fears of exposing shortcoming (Boice 1993) that they possess. Sometimes this is precipitated by a peer or chair's statement of devaluation and other times it is more reflective of a self assessed shortcoming. In either case, it can become debilitating and create a situation where the faculty member feels immobilized rather than energized to realistically assess whether the assessment is valid and what steps need to be taken. Others recount explicit racist or sexist comments that generated feelings of devaluation. Repeatedly being *placed* on "minority issue" committees or committees that are seen as traditionally women's concerns are viewed by many African American women to reinforce racist or sexist comments. One woman stated "if another one remarks that they can't believe I am pregnant again I'll scream, they see me as just another black, stupid baby machine." Such behavior and remarks reflect an androcentric and racist bias and creates an uncomfortable climate for these women, thus making it difficult for them to become a part of the departmental and the larger university community.

Further, African American women faculty members and other under represented groups often are burdened with heavy loads of committee work, university service and community work (Verrier 1992). This can add to the dissatisfaction that faculty members experience as they realize that this cuts into the valuable time they need to publish. And finally the difficulty in gaining the resources needed to further scholarship/research interest can be disheartening. Although grants are competitive in all disciplines, African American faculty often lack the assistance of their peers in developing, collaborating on, or seeking grant monies. Thus spending an extraordinary amount of time developing proposals alone and yielding little results.

The Tenure Process

The tenure process for many African American women and men is short circuited by prematurely dropping out of the system. Women report that it is sometimes preferable to drop out of the system if you feel you might have a problem, rather than to go through the public nature of the tenure process (Bronstein 1993).

University of Delaware has 27 African American faculty members out of 901 faculty, representing 2.9 percent of the total faculty. Of the tenured faculty, 2.2 percent are African American and of the tenured track 6.3 percent are African American. The number of male and female African American faculty are approximately equal and with such a small number no gender difference in seen within rank. Women, in general, at the University of Delaware like other women faculty are disproportionately at lower rank, however African Americans males and females are equally not present (Commission on the Status of Women, 1993). Reviewing the trends from 1987 to 1993, there is no significant increase in the number of actual African American faculty that acquired tenure status (See Table1.1). However, when you carefully track faculty retention over the years corresponding to the tenure process, it becomes apparent that individuals were more likely to drop out of the system than to stay and go up for tenure. Two reasons could drive this tendency. African American women and men could, as I suggested earlier, drop out of the system after a less than satisfying evaluation or a perception that they will not achieve tenure or faculty members could be recruited or choose to go on to another institution. Although this certainly happens in some cases, it is inconsistent with the overall tendency of poor retainment and tenuring of African American faculty across the nation (Johnsrud 1993; Touchton and Davis 1991). Thus they seem to be more likely to drop out of the tenure track academic community.

The tenure process requires that a faculty member have a documented record of scholarship, teaching, and service that is recognizable by the male defined university departmental culture. The establishment of such a record is not something that can be done quickly or without an understanding of what delineates the culture of the faculty member's department.

Keeping Records

Returning to the theme of critical periods for African American women faculty, preparation is extremely important in gaining tenure. Because it takes a documented record to achieve tenure, it is absolutely necessary that appropriate time is given to establishing this record. Teaching typically is on a predictable timed schedule. Thus faculty members teach on either the semester or quarter system as designated by their university system. Faculty members need to keep on file information concerning teaching for use in developing their dossier. Thus it becomes important to keep an organized per term record of what is taught, how many students were enrolled, a copy of syllabi, reading lists and course evaluations for later use. This record of teaching will save time later and give faculty members the documentation that they will need when it becomes time to put together materials for presentation.

Service commitments are less predictable than most teaching assignment and thus need a careful recording of these obligations. Responding to service commitments and keeping no record is a waste of time. It is very important to know how your department documents service and to maintain appropriate files. This record should at least include: what the service activity was (committee, presentation, workshop, etc.), when was service provided, and any letter documenting the event (letter thanking you for your contribution, a memo documenting the committee assignment, a report culminating from the committee assignment listing committee members, etc.).

Keeping adequate records is very important in both teaching and service because it is difficult and sometimes impossible to recreate the information months or even years after the assignment.

Strategies For Developing A Successful Public Accord

The most important factor in successfully achieving tenure is the development of a research agenda and the establishment of a publication record. The quicker a faculty member can begin to develop this record, the more secure you will be within your department and the more effectively you can demonstrate your record of publication.

Many scholars have examined the components that seem to be most important in developing a successful publication record (Verrier 1992; Phillip 1993). Most African American faculty do not enter systems where these components are readily available, thus it is important to cultivate such mechanisms quickly.

Probably the most commonly discussed strategy for success in the academy is a mentor (Fisher 1988; Johnsrud 1993; Olsen, Maple and Stage 1991; Sandler 1993; Wright and Wright 1987; Farley 1990). A mentor is an individual at a rank above the mentee who can act as a guide and an advocate for the African American faculty member. This person should not be chosen lightly and may not formally see themselves as a mentor. However, it is important that the relationship is mutual such that both are willing participants in the relationship (Fisher 1988). If this person is not within you department, it is necessary to have a supportive relationship with a departmental member above rank. This person can be used to check that the more general advice of your mentor fits the cultural norms of your department. Mentors can provide invaluable advice on how to acquire needed resources, how to develop linkages with faculty members with similar interest and information to assist new faculty members or less connected faculty members in understanding the university or departmental systems.

The chair of the faculty member's department is well placed to have the experiences and information that new faculty need. Thus this person can make an excellent mentor. Johnsrud (1993) describes the position of the departmental chair as one that can provide a sense of belonging, realistic information on career progress, a supportive collegial relationship and an insurance on the equity of resources for new faculty members. Additionally, chairs are aware of the cultural expectations of the department and can thus realistically provide African American faculty with needed information concerning the number of publications and the type of scholarship activities that are valued within the department. However chairs and other mentors must be able to understand the racism and sexism inherent in the system and to work toward a climate that eliminates these behaviors. Most certainly the androcentric academic climate is challenged by a diverse faculty. The chair of the department can be instrumental in changing the expectations and creating a climate where racism and sexism is not tolerated. A chair that is not capable of assisting new African American faculty in adjusting to the department will, of course, not make an effective mentor.

Locating and establishing individuals to collaborate with on research projects will maximize research efforts. The publication efforts of scholars that collaborate is typically three times that of researchers that publish alone (Welch 1990). Collaborating with peers both within your department or across campus can maximize faculty efforts (Clague 1992; Moses 1989). If these individuals are well matched, it can be an extremely productive relationship for all involved. Additionally, working with colleagues can benefit scholarly activities in two very important ways. This sharing of tasks can reduce the workload of individuals working together and collaboration can motivate and enhance the productivity and quality of scholarship. Long distance collaboration is sometimes chosen by faculty members. Once the team works out the logistics of transferring information, this relationship may also be highly productive.

In addition to these strategies it is extremely beneficial to establish or become a part of one or more supportive network. These networks can be broad based university or community groups or groups focused around a specific issue. Networks allow faculty members the benefits of groups of individuals that understand some, if not all, of the issues African American women faculty members face. Thus a university network of African American faculty and staff may be able to supply the support that is needed when a new faculty member experiences isolation as one of the few (if not only) African American faculty members within their department. Networks can also assist new faculty in obtaining culturally specific information, as well as providing some racial balance. Women studies faculty or broader women's networks can also furnish support for new African American women on campuses. Networks can assist in bridging the gap for new faculty members and provide supportive exchanges for African American women faculty.

Once a successful record of scholarship has been established, there is an important and absolutely necessary step that is commonly missed. This involves the presentation of materials for the dossier. Women faculty members often state that their scholarship will "stand on its own merit." In a fair system this kind of notion might be realistic, however in a system that is neither familiar, comfortable or supportive of African American women faculty, it is both naive and potentially lethal to invest in such a notion. Unless your research paradigms, questions, concerns and theories are 100 percent mainstream (which means male centered, based on white populations, and single focused) you have some explanations that need to be articulated within your dossier. The malice and devaluation that has often been demonstrated when criticizing African American scholarship is often exercised because the evaluation committees have no basis or framework to understand our scholarship. It is *absolutely* necessary to provide the elaboration for the various committees that will be reviewing the submitted work. The statement is not an apology, it is a statement of illumination, in the introductory section of the dossier and especially the section on research, where you make appropriate linkages for the reviewers. Describe how the submitted work is tied together, what the overriding goal of your research agenda is and how the submitted pieces address your research agenda. Do not assume that reviewers will understand your goals, they will not. Instead use this as an opportunity to tell your reviewers what you are doing within your research agenda. This will not only serve to maximize achieving tenure and promotion, but it will elevate your field by broadening its scope. The work of African American women and other people of color expands all disciplines. Those of us, who do research in areas that are central to our disciplines do it differently because of who we are and those of us that branch off into uncharted territory enlarge the scope and understanding of our fields. It is important to articulate a research agenda and to explain how your work addresses this agenda. In universities androcentric, white dominated environment not offering such clarification invites an unfavorable review of scholarship that does not fit "exactly" the mode of the existing academic culture.

Conclusions

Achieving tenure is not something that happens at the end of six years or so. It is a process of establishing yourself within a system that was not designed to accommodate African American women. Moreover, it is a system that has difficulty understanding the contribution of this group and must be educated to recognize that African American women's scholarship will advance the work of all disciples and foster the creation of a woman-centered university. The old system is challenged as more women of color are tenured. As tenured women, we can move to develop policies, tear down walls, and seek strategic positions so that we can make a difference in the world of education, knowledge, and action that African American students and scholars are drawn to. In order to provide leadership within the academic world, we must understand that world. The tenure process can be mastered, but only when we understand the process and steadfastly work to successfully maneuver the obstacles placed in our way. It is important to demystify the process, to conquer and achieve tenure, and to begin the process of creating universities that respond to, and reflect both women and men of all races and ethnic backgrounds.

Table 1.1
Full-Time Tenured Faculty by Sex, Ethnicity, and Tenure Status
Fall 1987 through 1993

Total Males   Total Females

Fall	Total	Males	White	Black	Hisp	Asian	Female	White	Black	Hisp	Asian
1987	512	429	403	6	3	16	83	76	4	2	1
1988	506	421	396	4	3	17	85	78	4	2	1
1989	537	439	408	5	4	21	98	98	90	5	1
1990	544	422	411	5	4	21	102	95	4	1	2
1991	559	446	414	4	3	24	113	105	5	0	3
1992	570	447	411	6	4	25	123	113	7	0	3
1993	591	468	428	6	4	29	123	113	7	0	3

Chapter 2

Women, Men, and Job Satisfaction in Academia: Perceptions of a Glass Ceiling Among Faculty

Juanita M. Firestone

This research investigates differences between men and women employed in the University of Texas (UT) system with respect to their level of job satisfaction. Results from initial analysis found that the average satisfaction scores for women, across various career stages and environments were consistently lower then the average scores for men (Faculty Quality Committee, 1995). Additionally, results from regression analyses confirmed that the coefficient for gender remained significant and negative even after controlling for tenure status, rank and whether the respondents worked in the academic or the health field environments. These findings suggest the need for further analysis of the data as a means of understanding differences in satisfaction between men and women teaching in the University of Texas system. The results have implications for men and women teaching at all state universities.

Background Literature

Job satisfaction is determined by a variety of factors. These factors include the nature of the job tasks (Kohn 1990; Miller 1980), technology (Blauner 1964; Braverman 1974; Form and McMillen 1983: 175), organizational characteristics (Katz and Kahn 1978), workers' participation in decision making (Bonjean et al., 1982), individual differences (Hodson 1989; Hall 1986), and prior expectations, (Kalleberg 1977), as well as needs for personal development (Argyris 1973; Herzberg 1966; McGregor 1967). The nature of job tasks involves several components. The first is autonomy, which refers to the degree to which an employee is able to control his or her own work as well as his/her relations with others (Kohn 1990). Greater autonomy leads to higher levels of satisfaction. Complexity of job tasks is the second component (Kohn 1990). Complex job responsibilities require more self direction. Individuals in positions involving complex tasks are "less psychologically distressed and more intellectually flexible" (Hodson and Sullivan 1995: 97). The final component is diversity of tasks. Repetitive work functions to increase alienation while diversity benefits workers both socially and psychologically.

Satisfaction may also be affected by technological developments. These developments may operate to either increase or decrease alienation (Hodson and Sullivan 1995: 100). If technology frees an individual to work on more diverse tasks, then alienation will decrease and satisfaction will increase. Conversely, if technology leads to more repetitive tasks, alienation will increase and satisfaction will decline (Hodson and Sullivan 1995).

Organizational structure and policies also strongly influence employee satisfaction. One element of organizational structure is its size. Small companies and small departments are preferred because larger structures increase isolation and create a sense of powerlessness in workers (Hodson 1984). In large organizations, "workers have difficulty in identifying the overall purpose and direction of their organization and in feeling that they are a significant part of that purpose" (Hodson and Sullivan 1995: 101). Policies such as pay and promotion issues also influence the degree of alienation an employee may experience. With regard to pay, it is essential that workers receive wages sufficient to meet their basic physiological needs for food and shelter. High pay, however, is not a determinant of employee satisfaction, but it is necessary to provide a living wage. Finally, promotion policies may create dissatisfaction in employees if there are no or few opportunities for advancement (Katz and Kahn 1978). "For a job to be fulfilling, it is necessary to have not only rewarding tasks, but also a meaningful career trajectory" (Hodson and

Sullivan 1995: 102). Lack of promotion opportunity can be especially debilitating if an employee's self-worth is tied into their career advancement (Hodson and Sullivan 1995). Employers must provide their workers "...the opportunity to grow and be at least reasonably in control of [their] own destinies" (DePree 1989: 23).

Employees who are blocked from the decision making process experience an increase in alienation (Bonjean et al., 1982). Participatory decision making can act to decrease that alienation. "Participation is the opportunity and responsibility to have a say in your job, to have influence over the management of organizational resources based on your own competence and your willingness to accept problem ownership. No one person is the expert at everything" (DePree 1989: 48). It is important for employers to remember that "by ourselves we suffer serious limitations. Together we can be something wonderful" (DePree 1989: 50).

The values of individual employees also influence levels of satisfaction in the work environment. How well these values conform to the requirements of the job determine how satisfied a worker will be. The greater the fit between values and requirements, the more highly satisfied an employee will be. Education is also a predictor of job satisfaction with more highly educated workers less satisfied because they have higher expectations regarding the "rewards a workplace should offer" (Hodson and Sullivan 1995: 106).

The experience of work differs by age, race, and gender. Research has shown that younger workers tend to be less satisfied than older workers (Hodson and Sullivan 1995). The reasons for this may be attributable to two different factors. First, younger workers tend to be better educated thus raising their expectations regarding the rewards of employment (Hall 1986). Second, older workers may have had more time to find positions more suited to their needs. Race and gender differences tend to be more complicated.

Women are more likely to be concentrated in lower paying jobs, doing more repetitive tasks, with fewer opportunities for advancement, and less opportunity to perform tasks involving high level skills (Hodson and Sullivan 1995). This carries over into academia where women are more likely than male counterparts to be employed in two-year institutions, in lower-tiered four-year institutions, and in non-tenure track positions in all institutions (Fox 1989; Grant and Ward 1996). This is compounded when women are also members of racial or ethnic minorities (Tuan et al., 1996). In spite of this, women consistently rate themselves as satisfied with their jobs as do men (Phelan et al., 1993). Part of this may be attributable to the fact that men and women evaluate their work experience using different standards (Crosby 1982; Hodson 1989; 1996). Just as men tend to compare themselves to other men, women tend to compare their positions relative to other women, thus lowering their achievement standards.

Like women, racial minorities are more likely to be concentrated in jobs that require fewer skills, pay more poorly, and are less rewarding. For example, in the university environment, while the many of the required skills may be the same across academic areas, women and racial/ethnic minorities tend to be clustered in the Humanities and Social Sciences where pay is lower and grants are more difficult to obtain (AAUP 1996; Grant and Ward 1996; Slater 1995). Unlike women, minority men register lower satisfaction ratings than white men(Form and Hanson 1985). This may be due to the fact that minorities compare themselves with the dominant group when making evaluations. Further, Hodson and Sullivan (1995: 103) state that minority workers "believe they should be treated equally with whites." Both factors combine to produce lower satisfaction levels because minorities do not perceive themselves as faring equitably against whites.

In a study of women and minority faculty, Olsen, Maple, and Stage (1995) found that both are susceptible to stereotypes. Even armed with information indicating that the work qualifications and backgrounds of men and women are identical, people perceive women as less competent than men (Etaugh 1984). Data suggest that women may also be experiencing the *Salieri effect* "whereby women are assessed by a dominant inner circle of men and fail to measure up because of their social status" (Clark and Corcoran 1986). The problem with the *Salieri effect* is that it "...is perhaps more insidious than overt discrimination because it allows women to enter academe while severely limiting opportunities for advancement" (Olsen et al., 1995: 270). The same problem may be occurring with minorities when institutions practice symbolic racism "which denounces overt forms of prejudice while denying access to resources, information, and sources of support (many of which are informal) essential to success" (Exum et al., 1983). A study conducted by the Association of Professional Women (APW) and released in 1995, compiled information from exit interviews administered to female faculty members who left the University of Texas at Dallas during 1992-1993. These findings tend to support the research discussed above. Although based on a small and not necessarily representative sample, (N=10) , the results are illustrative of the problems reported in other research. Females who left that university reported gender-specific harassment as well as having to deal with perceived stereotypes regarding women. These women perceived that they were excluded from decision making, were listened to less attentively because of their gender, and were excluded from social events where many policy decisions were made. Additionally, the women felt that they were not given access to resources readily available to male faculty members. Olsen, et al. (1995) found that access to resources varied by race and gender, with minority faculty reporting more recognition and support than women.

There is a behavioral component associated with every attitude. An individual's perception of job satisfaction may influence her or his behavior in a variety of ways. If employees feel that their needs are being met and that their own goals and values coincide with those of the employer, they (regardless of gender, race, ethnicity or age) will respond with greater commitment. If the job is perceived as rewarding, an employee will demonstrate greater enthusiasm in the performance of his/her duties. An enthusiastic employee is likely to make greater sacrifices for his/her employer including such things as working over-time without pay. Rather than being self-defeating, this behavior may actually help an individual become more self-actualized because it demonstrates that the goals, values, and identity of the person are realized through their work (Hodson and Sullivan 1995: 101). However, because of differences in socialization, perceptions about whether their goals and values coincide with the employer may differ for men and women. Thus, conditions that result in job satisfaction for male employees may or may not do the same for female employees.

Negative behaviors may be associated with low employee satisfaction. These include high levels of absenteeism, attrition, resistance and sabotage, and theft. All are responses to the alienation perceived by the individual and allow him/her to vent his/her frustration with the system. Negative behavior tends to occur when job rewards are low. If those rewards are high, employees may take a different approach and form unions to address those conditions that are perceived as unsatisfactory (Hodson and Sullivan 1995: 101). According to much of the recent literature on organizations, one important goal of an organization should be to ensure that all employees have every opportunity to fully realize their potential and become self-actualized human beings. In doing so, administrators of the organization should attempt to ensure that the needs of its workers, both physiological and psychological, are fully met. One measure of the success of an organization, particularly those which demand employees have high levels of education, is whether the individuals who work within it feel positive about *the extent to which we struggle to complete ourselves* and *the energy we devote to living up to our potential* (DePree 1989: 143). An organization that "frees its members to be their best" helps not only its workers, but also the organization itself in which it remains vital and responsive to a changing world (DePree 1989: 143). If in fact men's and women's perceptions differ, it becomes important to assess and understand those differences in order to attain that goal of all employees living up to their fullest potential.

Although explicitly directed at why women terminated employment, the findings from the UT Dallas study are relevant for discussing job satisfaction. Clearly, faculty who experience the problems associated with job dissatisfaction are more likely to leave. For example, an "overwhelming majority" of the women interviewed said they experienced one or more of the following:

* Witnessed or directly experienced gender-specific harassment
* Coped with negative stereotypes about women
* Said their personal life negatively affected the way they were treated
* Believed their workload was excessive compared to their colleagues
* Thought they were barred from some opportunities because of their sex

These findings suggest an organizational climate which is not perceived by female faculty as supportive in the same way that it is for men. The facts also point to an environment where women experienced feelings of alienation leading to powerlessness, self estrangement, meaninglessness, and isolation. In particular, the women reported a sense of isolation which is consistent with feeling job dissatisfaction. Furthermore, their reports of continuously coping with sexual harassment and stereotypes about women suggest that the

Salieri effect was experienced by these women. Thus, they were constantly assessed on the basis of their sex , rather than their job were operationalized using specific questions. Thus separate regressions were accomplished on general satisfaction, salary parity, performance and they were found lacking because they were women. Because this process is informal and covert, it is more difficult for women to cope with it, and thus is likely to contribute to lack of satisfaction on the job.

Data Analysis

The data used in this analysis were collected by the Faculty Quality Committee (FQC) of the University of Texas Faculty Advisory Council in 1990. The data include responses from 4,082 faculty from academic and health institutions in the University of Texas System. The overall response rate for the survey was 55 percent. The response rate from the Academic institutions was slightly higher (56 percent) than that from the Health institutions (53 percent).[1] Respondents included faculty from all institutions and all ranks within the system (Preliminary Faculty Satisfaction Survey Report, 1994).

In the original analysis, the items of the survey were "conceptually clustered into 12 composite satisfaction areas." Satisfaction scales, ranging from 1 (very dissatisfied) to 5 (very dissatisfied), were created for general satisfaction, intrinsic and extrinsic satisfaction, and satisfaction with academic freedom, self-actualization, collegiality, administration, faculty recognition and status, instructional support, compensation, salary, and research support.[2] Results from the initial analysis found that the average satisfaction scores for women, across various career stages and environments, were consistently lower then the average scores for men (Faculty Quality Committee, 1995: 56). Additionally, using OLS regression, the coefficient for gender remained significant and negative even after controlling for tenure status, rank and whether the respondents worked in the academic or the health environments.

This research performs additional analyses to better understand the original findings. To complete the follow-up analysis a variety of statistical techniques were utilized. Analyses performed on the original data included direct comparison of women's and men's scores on each the satisfaction measures, analysis of variance (ANOVA) and multiple regression (OLS).

The dependent variables utilized for the regression analysis were selected because of their importance in comparing women's and men's satisfaction.   The only one of the original scales included in the analysis was the general satisfaction scale. Other dependent variables salary competitiveness, and community respect.   Gender was introduced in stage one along with controls for rank, whether or not the individual has a Ph.D., tenure status, years at current institution, teaching load and, whether teaching load is primarily graduate or undergraduate.

The concept of a glass ceiling is an important one with respect to the experience of women in organizations. To test perceptions about a glass ceiling in the UT System institutions an index was created from the following variables measuring satisfaction with:

- Have time for professional goals
- Security of faculty position
- Chance to work with other professionals
- Chance for professional advancement
- Support received for research
- Staff and clerical support for instruction
- Amount of non-teaching duties

These variables seem to capture satisfaction or dissatisfaction with the types of structural supports which would be indicative of the perception of a glass ceiling.[3] While the index is not an exact measure of the environment in which a glass ceiling would occur, if women are more dissatisfied on these measures then men, they perceive less support and fewer opportunities for advancement.   A higher score on this index indicates more satisfaction, which suggests less of perception of the existence of a glass ceiling; lower satisfaction with the variables included is likely to indicate a perception that a glass ceiling exits.

In general, satisfaction is higher among both male and female faculty at the Health institutions than at the academic institutions. Additionally, females at the Health institutions more closely resemble men in levels of satisfaction.   However, there is greater variation between the sexes among faculty at the academic institutions.

Findings: Impacts of Gender and Race

There were significant differences based on the respondent's sex to "freedom to use own teaching methods", for both Academic and Health faculty. The relationship was stronger for Academic faculty, however. Interestingly, this is one question for which mean responses were higher among respondents from Academic institutions than among respondents from Health Institutions.   White males and females, as well as Hispanic female respondents from Academic institutions were most satisfied with a mean of 4.4 while Asian female respondents at Health institutions were the least satisfied at 3.6. Conversely, scores from faculty at Health institutions were highest with a mean of 4.2 for white and Hispanic females. However, they were lowest for both Asian males and females with a mean of 3.9. Race appears to have some impact on faculty satisfaction when controlling for sex of respondent, although the relationships are mainly of negligible or low strength. Its impact is seen more often among academic faculty.   Among males at Academic institutions scores on the question about security of faculty position were higher than those scores at Health institutions for all racial categories. Asian and other faculty at Academic institutions evidenced the highest score at 4.1. The lowest satisfaction rating was found among Black faculty at Health Institutions at 3.3. For women at Health institutions the pattern was the same, but there was greater variation between racial and ethnic groups.

Among faculty, white females displayed the greatest satisfaction at 3.7 while other females were least satisfied at 2.9.   White females at Health institutions evidenced the greatest satisfaction levels with a mean score of 3.5 and least satisfied were Hispanic females at 3.1.

Gender differences with the question about *satisfaction with salary* were marginally significant for both Academic and Health institutions. In this instance, Health faculty displayed greater satisfaction than Academic faculty. The most satisfied respondents were Black males at Health institutions with a score of 3.2 and the least satisfied were other females at Academic institutions with a mean score of 1.9.

Finally, there were minor gender differences to the question about *the way my chairperson responds to faculty* and *the importance given to teaching* among Academic faculty, but larger differences for faculty at Health institutions. There were no significant gender differences for either group for question 30: "the health and medical benefits for faculty". Both men and women at Academic institutions were either not sure or satisfied on this item. Both sexes at Health institutions responded that they were either satisfied or very satisfied to the same item.

Areas of Differences in Satisfaction by Gender

Relationships that showed significant gender differences for the Health institutions though not for the academic side include: *the amount of non-teaching duties; the orientation of new faculty members; and the quality of library support.* In each case, while statistically significant, the relationships are of negligible strength. With regard to non-teaching duties, Asian men had the highest levels of satisfaction at 3.7, while white and Hispanic women had the lowest levels with 3.2. Black men and women had equivalent mean satisfaction levels of 3.5. For satisfaction with faculty orientation, Black women had the highest mean score of 3.5, while Hispanic women had the lowest at 2.2. Mean satisfaction levels for men ranged from 3.0 for whites and Hispanics, to 3.1 for Blacks and Asians. Satisfaction with the quality of library support was most satisfactory for Black women at 4.2. Asian women and Black men were least happy with the quality of library support received indicated by their score of 3.7. Among the men, both Asian and White respondents had the highest satisfaction levels for this item at 4.1.

Significant gender differences were found for respondents from Academic institutions, but not from respondents at Health institutions to the following series of questions: *freedom to use professional competence; freedom to act consistently with my conscience; security of faculty position; importance given to research; my teaching load; chance for professional advancement; the way colleagues get along;; salary competitiveness with other public institutions; importance given to teaching; and participation of faculty in governance.* Most of these relationships were not very strong, with the exception of question 17 which asked about *the chances for professional advancement.* The range of responses was larger for this item with white males most satisfied at 3.4 with advancement opportunities and other females the least satisfied with a score of 2.5. With the exception of other males at 2.8, females were less likely to be satisfied with advancement opportunities than similarly situated males. While satisfaction with *security of faculty position*, evidenced only negligible gender differences, it is one of the items on which the overall mean satisfaction level was higher for Academic faculty than for Health faculty.

Academic Areas

Gender differences in faculty satisfaction also occurred within academic areas. Discipline membership appears to impact the satisfaction level of Academic faculty more often than Health faculty. Significant gender differences were found for Academic institutions but not for Health institutions on satisfaction with the following: *the level of respect for faculty in the community; the chance to do things for other people; the staff support for instruction; my status at the institution as a faculty member; and the feeling of accomplishment with my work.*

Satisfaction with *community respect* ranged from a high of 4.4 for males in Nursing to 3.3 for males in Math/Science and Arts and the Humanities, and females in both the Social Sciences and Arts and the Humanities. Among females, the highest satisfaction levels were found among females in Nursing at 4.2.

Satisfaction with *the opportunity to do things for others* ranged from 4.6, again for males in Nursing, to 3.4 for females in Business. Among males, those in Math/Science and Engineering have the lowest levels of satisfaction at 3.8. Among females, the highest levels of satisfaction were found in the disciplines of Nursing with a score of 4.2 and Engineering with a score of 4.3.

Staff support for instruction had a considerably lower range of mean scores. The highest score of 3.2 was evidenced by males of "other" races, and for females in Nursing. The lowest satisfaction level was 2.2 evidenced by females in Engineering. Females in Business also had comparatively low levels of satisfaction with mean scores of 2.4. Among males, those in Engineering had the lowest mean score at 2.

Gender differences for satisfaction with the *status of faculty members* at the respondents' institution were significant for faculty at Academic institutions, but not for those at Health institution. Mean satisfaction levels ranged from 3.7 for females in Nursing to 3.1 for both females in Allied Health and females in the Arts and Humanities. Among males, disciplines of Education and Engineering, along with the "Other" category had the highest mean score at 3.6, while males in the Social Sciences and Arts and Humanities had the lowest mean score at 3.3.

Satisfaction levels for achieving a sense of accomplishment with work showed little variation based on sex of respondent with one exception. Males in Nursing had a mean satisfaction score of 4.8. The next highest mean score was for males in Allied Health sciences which dropped all the way to 4.0. The lowest satisfaction score of 3.5 to this question was found among women in Engineering and Math/Sciences. The highest score among women was 3.9 for disciplines of Education, Nursing, and also for the "Other" category.

There were two areas where significant gender differences emerged for Health institutions regardless of discipline, but not for Academic institutions. Satisfaction with *the amount of non-teaching duties* had a small gender difference for respondents at Health institutions. With only one exception, scores were above 3.0. This exception was for males in Nursing who had a mean satisfaction level of 2.7. The highest score was 3.8 for men in Public Health. Among women, Graduate School faculty had the highest mean of 3.5 and Nursing faculty had the lowest mean of 3.0. There were also minor gender differences in satisfaction with *the way my performance is evaluated* among faculty at Health institutions. Scores ranged from 2.8 for females in Dental Schools to 3.3 for females in Nursing. Among males, scores ranged from 3.0 (Allied Health, Dental, and Nursing Schools) to 3.2 (Medical Schools).

Gender differences were larger among respondents from Academic institutions for several questions such as satisfaction with *having time to reach my professional goals; the security of my faculty position; the chance to work with other professionals; the way policies are put into practice; the way my colleagues get along together; and the retirement benefits for faculty*, all had negligible gender differences for Health faculty, but stronger differences for Academic faculty. Satisfaction with the way policies are put into place is another instance in which Academic gender differences were stronger than those from Health institutions. Male faculty in Nursing at Academic institutions were the most satisfied of any group with a score of 3.8 to that question. This is especially interesting in light of the fact that Male Nursing faculty at Health institutions had the lowest overall satisfaction score of 2.3 of any other group, whether male or female, at those facilities. The least satisfied group at Academic institutions were female Math/Science faculty with a mean score of 2.2.

Additionally, several questions regarding satisfaction with salary revealed relatively small gender differences among faculty at Health institutions, but had considerably more variation among respondents from Academic institutions, regardless of discipline. These include satisfaction with *my salary; the parity of faculty salary at my institution; and the competitiveness of faculty salary with other public universities.*

Female-Dominated Areas - Health Institutions

For respondents from Health institutions, academic discipline was dichotomized by dichotomizing Nursing and Public Health into one category and all other disciplines into another category.[4] In fact, fewer significant relationships occurred and the majority of those became weaker once the variable was dichotomized. Satisfaction with community respect is the only variable that became significant after dichotomizing and that was not significant when the full range of academic disciplines was retained. The new relationship, however, is not very strong. Males in Nursing/Public Health had a mean of 3.8 while Females had a mean of 3.9. Males and Females in all other disciplines had a mean satisfaction level of 3.7.

Impact of Rank and Tenure Status

In the area of academic rank, Professor and Associate Professor were grouped and re-coded to tenured positions, Assistant Professor was re-coded into tenure track positions, and Lecturer/Instructor and Other were re-coded into a non-tenure track category. The majority of significant relationships were of low or negligible strength. Satisfaction with *the security of my faculty position and the chances for professional advancement* both evidenced moderate gender differences for Health faculty regardless of rank. However, regardless of rank, large gender differences for Academic faculty were noted for *the security of my faculty position* and, smaller differences for *the chances for professional advancement.*

With regard to the security of faculty position, it is not surprising that the highest mean satisfaction scores were found among tenured

respondents.   Means were higher for both men and women at
Academic institution (Men = 4.3 and Women = 4.2) than Health
institutions (Men = 3.8 and Women = 3.9). Interestingly, tenure track
females at Academic institutions shared the same 2.9 mean as non-
tenure track females, which is lower than the mean for both tenure
track and non-tenure track males at 3.1. Among respondents at Health
institutions there was less variation within groups based on tenure
status and mean scores were consistent with what would be expected
.i. e., highest among tenure-track groups and lowest among those
respondents who were not in tenure eligible positions.

Results of the analysis for *chances for professional development*
indicated that tenured faculty were more satisfied than non-tenured
faculty at both Academic and Health institutions. Mean satisfaction
levels at Health institutions ranged from 3.6 for tenured males to 2.6
for non-tenured females whereas satisfaction levels for Academic
institutions ranged from 3.4 for tenured males to 3.0 for both non-
tenured males and females. With the exception of the non-tenured
Academic group, females of all tenure ranks at both Academic and
Health institutions are less satisfied than males with the opportunities
for professional advancement.   Satisfaction with *freedom to use
professional competence; individual salary; freedom to use own
teaching methods; amount of non-teaching duties; and, faculty
participation in faculty governance* evidenced significant gender
differences within academic rank for faculty at Health institutions, but
not for those at Academic institutions.   These relationships ranged
from negligible to low strength. Satisfaction with *community respect
for faculty; freedom to act consistently with my conscience; the way
colleagues get along; the competitiveness of salary with other public
institutions; and,   retirement benefits*   were significant for the
Academic group, but not for the Health group.   Although statistically
significant, the relationships were not very strong.

Satisfaction with salary, while only significant for respondents from
Health institutions, resulted in some interesting findings. As expected,
faculty tenured at Health institutions were most satisfied with their
salaries, while non-tenured faculty were the least satisfied. However,
non-tenured males were the most satisfied among the Academic
respondents.   Additionally, both tenured and non-tenured women at
academic institutions were less satisfied than those females in tenured
positions at Health institutions and men at all levels in both academic
and health institutions.

Satisfaction with salary; freedom to use professional judgment; and, *health and medical benefits* had stronger gender differences among Health faculty than Academic faculty. On *satisfaction with salary,* respondents at Health institutions were, on average, unsure while Academic respondents were more likely to claim dissatisfaction. Results for *freedom to use professional judgment,* indicated that most respondents of both genders and both Academic and Health institutions are satisfied. Finally, the mean scores for h*ealth and medical benefits,* indicated Academic respondents, regardless of gender were unsure of their satisfaction while Health respondents of both genders were more likely to state they were satisfied.

Gender differences on *satisfaction with teaching load,* while significant for both groups, were stronger for Academic faculty than for Health faculty. Overall, both men and women respondents at Health institutions were more likely to be satisfied while men and women at Academic institutions were more likely to be unsure of their satisfaction with their respective teaching loads.

The descriptive results show consistent, statistically significant gender differences in various measures of faculty satisfaction. While the differences are small in magnitude, they do suggest, however, that women faculty who responded to the survey may perceive an organizational climate that is not as supportive of their professional needs in the same way that it is for men. The next section investigates one possible source of women's perceptions.

Table 2.1
Proportion of Time Spent on Work Activities - Academic

	Males %	Females %	Eta
Teaching	47.0	53.0 t*	.12
Research	33.3	28.0*	.13
Univ. Service	18.4	17.5	.02
Community Service	09.8	10.5	.03
Total	108.9	109.0	

$* = P < .05$

Time Allocation

Differences in reported time distributions between men and women follow lines established in the literature reviewed. Women in academic settings report spending a significantly larger proportion of time on teaching and a significantly smaller proportion of time on research than their male colleagues (Table 2.1). While the women also reported a slightly larger proportion of time in university service than men, and the men reported a slightly larger proportion of time in community service than women, these differences were not statistically significant. Further analysis revealed that the largest disparities between men and women on proportions of time spent on teaching (Females: 43.06 percent; Males: 32.4 percent), university service (Females: 28.03 percent; Males: 23.85 percent), and community service (Females: 13 percent; Males: 9.54 percent) occurred among individuals who reported the lowest typical teaching load.[5] Men and women reporting higher typical teaching loads noted similar time allocations. Men with lower teaching loads report a larger proportion of their time is spent on research (43.5 percent) than do comparably situated women (32.23 percent). Interestingly, the totals add up to more than 100 percent of time. It could be that individuals felt unable to distribute their time based on a simple percentage distribution. In most university settings, the proportion of time individuals spend on each activity depends on a variety of factors. For example, proportion of time spent on teaching can vary depending on whether it is examination time in a course, whether the course is undergraduate or graduate, and the number of students in the class, just to mention a few. Proportion of time on research is impacted by stage of research-- whether at the beginning stage of a research project, or whether a project has just been completed.

Proportion of time in University service can depend on the committee structure and the charge of the various committees. Community service can also vary widely often depending on public demand.

Looking at Health Institutions, we see that women report spending a significantly larger proportion of time in non-patient related teaching than men, while men reported spending a significantly larger proportion of time on research (Table 2.2). Women also reported spending a slightly larger proportion of time in patient related teaching, non-teaching patient care, and administrative service than male colleagues, but the differences were not statistically significant. The men reported spending a slightly larger proportion of time in community service than their female colleagues. This difference was not statistically significant. More detailed examination showed that among those reporting the highest typical teaching load, men reported spending a larger proportion of time in patient related teaching (56.1 percent) than women (46.7 percent). Among those reporting the lowest typical teaching loads, women reported spending a larger proportion of time on non-teaching patient care (32.5 percent) and administrative service (27.4 percent) compared to men (27.1 percent; 18.2 percent respectively). The most dramatic difference occurred among individuals who reported their typical teaching load as 9 hours, where men reported spending 51.4 percent of their time on research, while women reported spending 16.8 percent of their time on research. Note that the proportion of time respondents from Health Institutions reported is dramatically higher than 100 percent. Once again, this could be indicative of individuals having difficulty allocating time based on simple percentages.

Table 2.2
Proportion of Time Spent on Work Activities - Health

	Males %	Females %	Eta
Patient Related Teaching	38.4	39.1	.01
Non-Patient Related Teaching	17.7	24.6*	.10
Non-Teaching Patient Care	27.5	30.6	.04
Research	40.5	35.9*	.05
Administrative Service	18.3	21.5	.04
Community Service	09.6	08.9	.01
Total	152.0	160.6	

* + P < .05

Regression Findings

The regression results reinforce the importance of gender with respect to understanding gender differences in satisfaction. In the bi-variate relationships, women are less satisfied with respect to each of the dependent variables in both the Academic and the Health institutions.   Importantly, for the Academic institutions the impact of being female is not explained away in any of the equations when the other controls are introduced to equalize experience across institutions. For the health institutions, gender remains significant for salary parity after the controls are entered into the equations, but is no longer a significant predictor of general satisfaction, satisfaction with salary competitiveness, or community respect.

For the academic institutions, multiple regression (OLS) was used to determine the impact of gender on *general satisfaction, satisfaction with salary parity, satisfaction with competitiveness of salary with other public institutions,* and *satisfaction with community respect* after equalizing for differences in tenure status, rank, teaching load, and years at current institution across institutions.   Thus, gender remains significant even when the structural variables which should account for such differences remain constant.   In all cases women remain less satisfied than male counterparts, and the results are statistically significant.   These findings are particularly salient for perceptions about salary competitiveness and salary parity: women are less satisfied than male colleagues even after controlling for rank, tenure status, teaching load, and years at the institution are controlled.   Note that for the equation predicting satisfaction with salary parity, gender has the second strongest impact (Beta= -.12)

For the Health institutions, once rank, tenure status, teaching load, and years at the institution were controlled, gender was no longer a significant predictor of general satisfaction, satisfaction with competitiveness of salary with other public institutions, and satisfaction with community respect. However, gender, which was not significant at the bi-variate level, became a significant predictor of satisfaction with salary parity.   This suggests that women's dissatisfaction with salary parity may be due their different status and position within the various institutions.   Similarly to the academic institutions, dissatisfaction with salary parity is not accounted for when rank, tenure, teaching load, and years at current institution are equalized across institutions.

Glass Ceiling

Regression results predicting scores on the glass ceiling index for the academic institutions verify that being female is associated with a lower score on the glass ceiling index and a higher likelihood of perceiving a glass ceiling. Furthermore, gender remains significant after introducing controls for rank, teaching load, type of teaching, years at institution and perceptions about salary parity. For health institutions, regression results also predict a lower score for woman. However, when the controls for rank, teaching load, type of teaching, years at institution and perceptions about salary parity are introduced, gender becomes statistically non-significant, suggesting that perceptions about structural inequalities rather than perceptions of a glass ceiling prevail.

The perception of a glass ceiling at health institutions seems to be explained by differences in respondent's individual positions within the institutions. This suggests that perceptions about the existence of a glass ceiling may be explained by differences in status between men and women. However, for the academic institutions, gender remains an important factor in perceptions about a glass ceiling even when differences in individual positions are held constant. Thus, when matched for rank, teaching load, type of teaching, years at institution, and perceptions about salary parity, women remain more likely to perceive a glass ceiling than men, suggesting that they are likely to actually experience one.

Conclusions and Policy Recommendations

The cross-tabular analyses and analysis of variance (ANOVA) completed for this report show that women are less satisfied than their male counterparts in the UT system. The gap between their levels of satisfaction varies depending on the specific topic with the largest difference for both health and academic institutions occurring on satisfaction with salary parity. Multivariate regression analyses (OLS) reinforced these findings. For academic institutions, gender remained a significant predictor of general satisfaction, satisfaction with salary parity, salary competitiveness, and community respect for academic institutions when controls for rank, tenure status, teaching load, type of teaching, whether or not respondent had earned a Ph.D., and years at institution were controlled. In all cases women were less satisfied than men. For the health institutions, gender remained a significant predictor only of satisfaction with salary parity after controlling for the status and structural variables. Again, women were less satisfied than male colleagues.

An analysis of reported time distributions provided additional information. In general, women in academic settings reported spending a larger proportion of their time in teaching and service than their male colleagues, while men reported spending a larger proportion of their time in research. Women in health institutions reported spending more time in non-teaching patient care and university service than men, while the men reported spending more time in patient-related teaching, research and community service. When refined further, interesting patterns emerged. Among those in academic institutions reporting the lowest teaching load, women report spending a larger proportion of their time in teaching, university service, and community service, while men reported spending more time in research. Among those in health institutions reporting the highest teaching loads, men report spending a larger proportion of time in patient-related teaching. At the lowest reported teaching loads, women report spending a larger proportion of time in non-teaching patient care and administrative service. Perhaps most interesting, among those individuals reporting an average teaching load of 9 hours, men report spending 51.4 percent of their time in research, while the women reported spending 17.8 percent of their time in research.

The analyses of an index designed to measure perceptions of the presence of a glass ceiling revealed that in both academic and health institutions, women were more likely than men to perceive a lack of support and limited opportunities for advancement. This remained true for the academic side even when status and position controls were introduced. However, gender became non-significant for the health side when the same controls were introduced. Thus while women in both arenas are more likely than men to perceive a glass ceiling, for women in health institutions, this perception may derive from status and position differences between men and women. On the other hand, women in academic institutions seem likely to actually experience a glass ceiling.

These findings strongly support two policy recommendations. First salary inequities not accounted for by rank, years at institution, tenure, and performance should be located and remedied. Second, a more structured approach to mentoring new faculty in general, and women in particular, should be developed. This process should guide all faculty, but especially those at research centered institutions to keep service and teaching responsibilities in perspective relative to research expectations. Finally, the data used in this report contained no information regarding sexism or sexual harassment. However, the findings suggest that future investigations on these issues could provide meaningful input into policies designed to improve the satisfaction of women, at least in the UT system.

Table 2.3
Analysis of Perceptions of the Existence of a Glass Ceiling

	Academic Institutions		Health Institutions	
	B	Beta	b	Beta
	Std. error		Std. error	
Female	-.07**	-.04**	.06	.04
	(.03)		(.04)	
Undergraduate Teaching	.04	.03	-03	-.01
	(.03)		(.07)	
Graduate Teaching	.06	.03	-.01	-.01
	(.04)		(.04)	
Teaching Load	-.09*	-.13*	-.09*	-.14*
	(.02)		(.02)	
Assistant Professor	-.14*	.09*	-.25*	-.17*
	(.07)		(.06)	
Associate Professor	-.10*	.03*	-.21*	-.14*
	(.04)		(.04)	
Ph. D.	-.04	-.02	-.01	-.004
	(.05)		(.05)	
Tenured	.08	.05	.14*	.10*
	(.07)		(.05)	
Years at Institution	.04*	.09*	-.002	-.01
	(.01)		(.01)	
Salary Parity	.21*	.33*	.27*	.44*
	(.01)		(.01)	
Constant	2.87		2.99	
Adjusted R^2	.20		.28	

*p<.01; **p<.05, one-tailed test

Notes

1. A detailed description of original sampling procedure and return rates by gender, rank, race/ethnicity, and tenure status are available upon request.

2. A detailed description of the original scales and the procedures for their development are available upon request.

3. Reliability (alpha) for index is .7545.

4. Because Nursing/Public Health are female-dominated its logical that greater gender differences might be observed after controlling for such gender segregation within disciplines.

5. Teaching loads varied from 3 hours per semester to 15 hours per semester depending on type of institution and the particular campus.

The author would like to thank Richard J. Harris and Mary J. Bollinger for their assistance in this research and the Office of the Chancellor for providing funding for the original report.

Chapter 3

The Academy: Vehicle for Gender Equity and Cultural Justice

Kenneth L. Miller, Susan M. Miller, and Gwen Schroth

This chapter addresses two seemingly incongruous aspects of the American Academy in a cultural context. The first is that institutions of higher learning are barometers of larger cultural climates in which they exist. Cultural dynamics and issues observed on broad social, political, and economic landscapes in the United States are mirrored in cultural dynamics observed on our nation's campuses. Of particular note are parallels in the prevalence of gender bias, discrimination, and inequities that hamper the frequently voiced goals of equality and "justice for all" in both of these climates.

The second major point regarding the Academy in a larger cultural context is that its unique institutional status, roles, and functions make it an ideal vehicle to create and promote cultural justice. Institutions of higher learning in the United States enjoy worldwide acclaim for the quality of their educational programs and for the value placed upon their graduates. The high status accorded colleges and universities by the international community stems, in part, from the climate in which educational programs are provided. Public colleges and universities are mandated to uphold certain democratic ideals, valued by many nations, in the process of educating their students. Under federal laws, they are forbidden to discriminate against persons based on sex, race, and other cultural variables in order to provide equal access and opportunities to all. The intent of such legislation is to produce an educated citizenry that will, at least in theory, perpetuate the ideals of equality and fairness in society at-large. If the Academy can achieve a culture-fair learning environment, unencumbered by the bias, discrimination, and inequities that characterize the larger culture in which it exists, it may lay legitimate claim to be an "equalizing" force in the American meritocracy; a model of cultural justice.

This chapter focuses on women's issues in both social and academic arenas. More precisely, it examines the dynamics of gender bias and discrimination and introduces a model to promote gender equity and justice in our nation's colleges and universities. This examination begins in Section II by defining cultural terms used throughout the chapter. Section III explores the prevalence of gender bias and discrimination in the United States, highlighting the ways in which these phenomena have shaped our cultural lens to become indelible aspects of our social institutions. Section IV examines gender bias and discrimination on our nation's campuses, focusing on the vehicles by which they are made manifest: access, institutional policies and practices, campus climate, and faculty. In Section V, a model for creating a gender-fair academic environment is presented. The chapter concludes with a summary of main points and a discussion of choices for administrators and faculty.

Defining the Cultural and Gender Playing Field

The overlapping use and misuse of cultural terminology suggests that discussions of cultural or gender issues begin with a definition of terms. Terms to be defined in this section include: culture, subculture, gender, sex, sexual orientation, bias, prejudice, discrimination, sexism, heterosexism, gender stereotyping, sexual harassment, gender harassment, multicultural education, gender-fairness, and gender competence.

Culture comprises the values, beliefs, ideologies, skills, tools, and customs held by persons in various racial, religious, or social groups as fundamental and necessary for effective social functioning. Culture serves as a roadmap for behavior (McDermott et al., 1980; Sue and Sue 1990). In comparison, subculture refers to common knowledge, values, customs, and behaviors that guide life in smaller social groups such as neighborhoods, military organizations, or groups that share school or work experiences (McDermott et al., 1980).

Gender refers to characteristics that differentiate the lives of males and females and which support the unique orientations of each toward problems and solutions (Baruth and Manning 1991). Gender is a psychological phenomenon that is culturally determined. That is, males and females are culturally conditioned to adopt behaviors, attitudes, and activities considered appropriate and desirable (i.e., masculine or feminine) for their sex (Hirsch et al., 1991). In this manner, gender is differentiated from sex, a biological phenomenon. Sexual orientation refers to an individual's preference for sexual activity with people of the opposite sex (i.e., heterosexuality), the same sex (i.e., homosexuality), or both sexes (i.e., bisexuality) (Hirsch et al., 1991).

Bias is a tendency, strong inclination of the mind, or a preconceived opinion about something or someone that prevents unprejudiced consideration of a question. Bias may be positive or negative in that it may favor or run contrary to an idea or a group (Flexner and Hauck 1993). Prejudice implies a hostile opinion about a person or group of persons. Prejudice is socially/culturally learned and is usually the result of misconception, misinterpretation, and rigid generalizations (Hirsch et al., 1991). Prejudice implies a judgment more unreasonable than bias (Flexner and Hauck 1993). Discrimination refers to personal or institutional belief systems and behaviors directed against individuals or groups based upon their race (racism), sex (sexism), sexual orientation (heterosexism), social class (classism), or other perceived differences (Nieto 1992).

Sexism refers to personal and institutional beliefs systems and behaviors directed against individuals or groups of people based on their sex (Nieto 1992). It is based on beliefs that one sex, usually the male, is naturally superior to the other and that this group should dominate critical dimensions of economic, political, and social life (Hirsch et al., 1991). Heterosexism is discrimination against gay men and lesbians (Nieto 1992).

Gender stereotyping includes both descriptive and prescriptive components. The descriptive component consists of attributes that comprise what people consider the typical group member to be like. The descriptive component of the female stereotype includes the attributes, "emotional, weak, dependent, passive, uncompetitive, and unconfident" (Fiske and Stevens 1993: 179). The prescriptive component of a stereotype is comprised of behaviors that people deem to be suitable for the target group: beliefs about behaviors that a member of the target group should exhibit. The female stereotype includes the prescriptive behaviors, "A woman should have good interpersonal skills, she should be passive and docile, and she should cooperate with others" (Fiske and Stevens 1993: 179).

Sexual harassment includes unwelcome sexual advances, requests for sexual favors, other physical and verbal conduct of a sexual nature when (a) submission to such conduct is made either explicitly or implicitly a term or condition of an individual's employment or educational benefits or services, (b) submission to or rejection of such conduct by an individual is used as the basis for academic or employment decisions affecting the individual or, (c) such conduct has the purpose or effect of unreasonably interfering with an individual's academic or professional performance or creating an intimidating, hostile, or offensive employment or educational environment (University of Hawaii, 1991, Office of Equal Employment Opportunity). Sexual harassment is a form of sex discrimination.

Gender harassment refers to harassment that "...is not sexual, and is used to enforce traditional gender roles, or in response to the violation of these roles. This form of harassment may also aim to undermine women's attempts at gaining power or to describe that power as illegitimately obtained or exercised" (Miller, L. 1997: 35). She offered as examples of gender harassment, men voicing that "women can't drive trucks" in the presence of women truck drivers or refusing to follow a female supervisor's orders simply because of her sex. Gender harassment is often subtle and impossible to trace, making attempts to regulate it extremely difficult.

Gender bias and discrimination cannot be fully understood outside of the power dynamics that drives them. These phenomena are all grounded in attempts to legitimize the power of one person or group over another (i.e., typically men over women) for some type of gain. If biased beliefs and discriminatory behaviors can be promoted as "acceptable" forms of human exchange, the inevitable result is legal or cultural codification of these phenomena (e.g., failure to punish rapists, wage disparities, the "glass ceiling"). Through these processes of social reinforcement, legitimacy is bestowed on both the practices that systematically deprive women to the benefit of men and on the belief systems that drive them. In this manner, male dominance is legitimized and institutionalized.

Multicultural education is a process of comprehensive education that challenges and rejects racism and the myriad forms of discrimination that exist in social institutions and in society-at-large. Multicultural education accepts and affirms the cultural pluralism that individuals, communities, and society represent. It promotes awareness of and respect for differences based on race, ethnicity, religion, sex, social class, sexual orientation, and all cultural distinctions (Nieto 1992).

Gender-fairness refers to personal and institutional beliefs, values, attitudes, views, judgments, policies, practices, and programs that reflect and promote acknowledgement of, respect for, and inclusion of the ideas, customs, traditions, norms, and practices of both women and men in the day-to-day functioning of a social unit. Gender-fair policies and practices are devoid of bias, prejudice, discrimination, and harassment. They promote equal opportunities for both men and women.

Adapted from a definition of cultural competence by Miller, Miller, and Gwaltney (1998: 39), the authors define gender competence as

> "the extent to which an individual is: (a) free of gender-biased attitudes and discriminatory behaviors, (b) aware of self as a gendered being in relation to one's own and the opposite sex, (c) knowledgeable of one's own and opposite sex dynamics and issues, (d) respectful of gender differences, and (e) skilled in the application of gender knowledge, particularly as it relates to communication and relationship building" .

Gender Bias and Discrimination in the United States

Gender stereotyping, bias, discrimination, inequities, and harassment are long-standing features of American society. Hundreds of research articles and books have documented the existence of these problems throughout American history. Rohrbaugh (1979) and Ruble and Ruble (1982) described how women have been subtyped to yield stereotypes that range from love goddesses to wholesome mother figures to inferior and evil creatures. Fiske and Stevens (1993) noted that such stereotypes are based on dramatic power differences in which men (in the current power structure) exercise control over women's outcomes. The majority of sex discrimination in the United States continues to occur against women (McWhirter 1997) and dramatic gender inequities still exist despite improvements in the status of women in recent decades (Moyer 1997).

Researchers have also examined gender bias and discrimination in the context of other cultural factors. Alexander (1995) documented the plight of American black women during the past 350 years who have been seen primarily as "...sexual beings who have no modesty, virtue, or intelligence, and little claim to respect or power" (p. 5). A 1992 American Association of University Women (AAUW) report revealed that minority girls continue to face particularly severe obstacles in school because of the need to confront both sexism and racism. Continued reports of racism, sexism, and classism in the United States (McWhirter 1997) support the argument that gender bias and discrimination cannot be fully understood outside of the context of other cultural variables.

Numerous studies document the prevalence and underlying causes of gender bias and discrimination in American social institutions. American public schools have been a primary target of such investigations. Selected findings reveal that all girls confront obstacles to equitable participation in school and society (AAUW, 1992) and 80 percent of students in grades eight through eleven have experienced some form of school-based sexual harassment (AAUW, 1993). Norrell and Norrell (1996) reported that some university policies may discriminate unfairly against women.

Another major institution targeted for the study of gender bias and discrimination has been the workplace. Studies have revealed that females anticipate more barriers to future employment than their male counterparts (McWhirter 1997). They also reveal that more effective work behaviors are attributed to men than to women due to a systematic response bias (Martell 1996). Moreover, much discrimination against women is based on stereotypes and is manifested through biased treatment by male co-workers (Naff 1995), and stereotyping is expected to limit employment opportunities for women in the future (Owen and Toder 1993). Additional findings include underrepresentation of women in top management positions (Fischer 1992) dramatically lower average incomes for women than men, and sexual segregation in many employment fields (Oskamp and Costanzo 1993). It is noteworthy that these relatively recent research findings are consistent with those of studies conducted thirty years ago.

Moyer (1997) reported results of two gender-related studies on the American media. The first revealed that 85 percent of front page stories in major American newspapers were about men. The second study was based on a random sample of 50 pages from the *Cambridge Dictionary of American Biography* (Bowman 1995) and showed that men accounted for 88 percent of the entries per page. These findings suggest that certain print media provide limited access to information about women.

L. Miller (1997) reported that gender harassment is more prevalent than sexual harassment in the United States Army and concluded that it is likely to persist, if not, to increase in the future. Stepnick and Orcutt (1996) reported that gender-biased behavior is pervasive in the practice of law in America. The authors noted that harassment, gender discrimination, and demeaning treatment of women in courtrooms and other legal settings is widespread. A report by Sprock and Yoder (1997) revealed that research on the detection and diagnosis of depression suggested both overdiagnosis bias for women and underdiagnosis bias for men.

Violence against women in the United States is ubiquitous. Bergmann (1986) pointed out that while America did not invent misogyny, neither did we refuse it entry at our shores. Although there is public recognition of the occurrence of acquaintance rape, Spence (1993) suggests that it is not wholehearted. Rape is not only a pervasive fact of American life, but also is its incidence growing rapidly. Between 1973 and 1993, there was an 88 percent increase in the rate of forcible rape per 100,000 inhabitants. There are at least 105,000 and perhaps more than 630,000 rapes committed annually in the United States. Over a twenty-year period, nearly 10 percent of the female population of the United States was raped (Buchwald et al., 1993). Despite these horrendous statistics, only one in 100 rapists is sentenced to more than one year in prison and nearly a quarter of convicted rapists are released on probation (Report of the Majority Staff of the Senate Judiciary Committee 1993).

Violence against women is sometimes subtle, yet it affects their lives in profound and devastating ways. Approximately 16,000 women have abortions each year as a result of rape or incest (The Alan Guttmacher Institute 1993). During the last 20 years, anti-abortion terrorists have been responsible for six murders, 15 attempted murders, 200 bombings and arsons, 72 attempted arsons, 750 death and bomb threats, and hundreds of acts of vandalism, intimidation, stalking and burglary (Clarkson 1998).

Hate crimes against gays and lesbians increased 260 percent between 1988 and 1996. In 1996, a minimum of 21 men and women were murdered because of their sexual orientation. Gays and lesbians are attacked six times more often in bias-motivated crimes than Jews or Hispanics and twice as frequently as Blacks. Despite the viciousness and brutality of these crimes, few cases are brought to court (Southern Poverty Law Center 1997).

Long range prospects for ameliorating the problems of gender bias, discrimination, and hatred are bleak. Sex discrimination against women in the workplace is likely to increase (Valentine and Mosley 1998) as is gender harassment in the United States Army (L. Miller 1997). The prospects for equal treatment of women in legal settings will hinge on fundamental structural change in the composition of the judiciary and in the law itself (Stepnick and Orcutt 1996), neither of which seems plausible. Acquaintance rape and sexual discrimination are likely to remain tragic features of the American landscape (Spence 1993) and America will continue to exist as a rape culture until society chooses to eradicate the sources of sexual violence (Buchwald et al., 1993). Given these circumstances, the authors turn their attention to the academy as both a microcosm of gender inequity and a vehicle for promoting gender equity and cultural justice.

Gender Bias and Discrimination in the Academy

The academy's treatment of women has largely paralleled that of the academy's relationship with individuals from other cultural groups (i.e., minorities and lower SES groups). Undeniably, the university serves as a gatekeeper in maintaining the status quo. Historically, it has excluded minorities, women, and the lower socioeconomic class. Paradoxically, it has provided a means of upward mobility for these same groups.

The women who comprise the majority of students on today's campuses are a diverse group. Precipitated by the civil rights movement of the 1960's, changes in social norms and expectations backed by federal mandates and financing has altered the landscape of the modern campus. As Pearson, Shavlik, and Touchton (1989) noted, college is no longer the sole domain of the elite few middle and upper class students who populated campuses a century ago. Today, a large number of high-school graduates attend two-year or four-year institutions. The student body includes individuals from lower and working class backgrounds and individuals who are diverse with regard to race, ethnic group, age, sexual preference, religion, and worldview (Pearson et al., 1989). Women who enter the ivory tower are subject to the long-standing secondary role that women have held in the academy. As women of color, as lower and working class women, as older women, as lesbians, they are also subjected to the constraints that the academy has placed on these groups. Any discussion of women and higher education must include personally and socially defining dimensions such as race, sexual orientation, and social class.

There are several methods for examining the nature and extent of sexism and gender inequity in higher education. One approach is to use access (i.e., enrollment) and attainment (degree status and financial outcomes) as indicators of equity. Research on institutional policies and practices has examined patterns in hiring, promotion and administrative procedures (i.e., maternity leave, tenure) that place female faculty at a disadvantage. Research on institutional sexism includes studies of sexual harassment and campus rape, which are also visible indicators of the chilly campus climate that women encounter. Research into the nature and extent of this chilly climate include studies that examine the experiences of female students as they live, study, and learn on campus. These studies examine overt and covert sexism that women encounter, differences in academic support and treatment, and the cumulative effects of this climate on self-esteem, self-confidence, and cognitive development. Finally, extending across these indicators are questions about the role of the most powerful members in the academy: faculty and administrators. These indicators are addressed in the following discussion.

Equity as Access

Those who view the academy as an advocate for social justice note the rapid rate of gain in enrollment made by women, who now comprise the majority of the student population. This view is akin to the belief that social justice is achieved by providing an "even playing field," thereby providing equal access to opportunities and outcomes. A different perspective focuses on equity in outcomes. This view holds that a just academy is one that results in equitable occupations, lifestyles, and financial rewards that are not based on gender.

Judging higher education from a perspective of access (i.e., enrollment) can lead to a view of the academy as an advocate for social change. But a closer scrutiny of enrollment patterns, persistence in higher education, and levels of attainment is likely to yield a view of the academy as social gatekeeper. The distinction is even more relevant when 2-year institutions are considered (Lin and Vogt 1996).

If access (i.e., enrollment) is a used as a barometer of social change, then a comparison of today's campus with one a century ago suggests that academia has risen to higher standards. A visitor to a modern campus would find an equal number of female and male students and a large, though non-representative, number of women (and men) of color and from lower and working class backgrounds. Gone are cultural norms of the last century, which proclaimed that the education of women created "monstrosities" (Sadker and Sadker 1995).

Women's entry into academia paralleled women's entry into society at large. The doors to education were virtually closed to the early American women who struggled to open them. As women pursued entry into traditionally male institutions, they also created their own institutions to which they held the key (Solomon 1985). By 1900, 19 percent of college graduates were women (Sadker and Sadker 1995). Resistance on both sides of the tower door continued into this century. In 1870, almost 60 percent of higher education institutions did not admit women, by 1957 this number was 13 percent (Solomon 1985).

Although women made steady but erratic gains in enrollment during the first half of this century, they accounted for almost 80 percent of enrollment gains from 1970 to 1985 (Chamberlain 1991). The 1960's civil rights movement brought increased social awareness of gender discrimination and the rise of national women's organizations (Chamberlain 1991). In the 1970's awareness transformed into legislation such as Title IX of the 1972 Higher Education Amendments to the Civil Right Act of 1964 which prohibited sex discrimination in any federally-funded educational program. Supported by the Women's Educational Equity Act, Title IX was a lever that tipped the equity scale (Sadker and Sadker 1995). Higher education heard the legislative message and institutions began visible, if not thorough, housecleaning to eradicate the odor of overt sexism (Chamberlain 1991).

The early 1980's marked a turning point in the relationship the academy had with those it had previously excluded.   In 1980-1981, more women (50.3 percent) than men earned master's degrees.   The following year more women (50.3 percent) than men earned undergraduate degrees.   This trend has continued; in 1991-92, women earned 54.1 percent of all masters' degrees and 54.2 percent of undergraduate degrees (National Center for Educational Statistics 1994).   Ironically, during this time period, changes in the political landscape saw federal equity projects and equity legislation lose financing and power (Sadker and Sadker 1995).   Concomitantly, alarmed by the large number of female students enrolled on their campuses, some institutions sought ways to limit their number (Chamberlain 1991; Sadker and Sadker 1995).

If equity is defined as access, then the roughly equal number of women and men currently enrolled in institutions of higher education signals success.   However, justice is not so easily beguiled; equality is an exacting, yet subtle phenomenon.   Although women and men enter institutions of higher education in equal numbers, they enter through different doors that lead to dissimilar opportunities, occupations and financial outcomes.   Women are more likely to attend 2-year than 4-year institutions (Lee et al., 1993; National Center for Educational Statistics 1992).   Women enrolled in 2-year institutions are less likely than men to transfer to 4-year institutions and subsequently to earn a bachelor's degree (Lee et al., 1993).   This disproportionate representation is even more dramatic for minority women (Lee et al., 1993; National Center for Educational Statistics 1992).   The gender gap in salary for college graduates begins to widen for graduates of 2-year institutions (Lin and Vogt 1996).   Female, minority, older, and low-income students are over-represented in less prestigious institutions, a pattern that translates into real world inequalities in occupational status and salary.

Men and women enter the same institutions, but they enter into different worlds.   Women may equal men in enrollment, but their educational experience is still unequal.   Sadker and Sadker (1995) coined the term "glass wall" (p.17) to describe the partition that separates the college experience of the female student from that of her male counterpart.   Women are over-represented in less prestigious and less financially rewarding "feminine" disciplines such as education and communication.   In contrast, men are over-represented in the more prestigious hard sciences (Chamberlain 1991; Sadker and Sadker 1995). The increased enrollment of women in recent decades has done little to change this disproportion.

Rather, for some disciplines, segregation by sex has risen. In 1971-1972 women earned 74.1 percent of all bachelor's degrees awarded in education, twenty years later this number grew to 79 percent. In the same year women earned only 14 percent of bachelor's degrees in engineering; 28.7 percent in computer and information sciences; and 32.6 percent in the physical sciences (National Center for Education Statistics 1994).

In graduate school the glass turns opaque. Historically, women have been under-represented in doctoral and professional programs. However, the recent enrollment gains noted above have slowly translated to more women in these programs. In 1889, women earned only 1.3 percent of all doctorates awarded; in 1961, only 3 percent of all professional degrees were awarded to women. Remarkably, given these figures, in the year 2001 women are projected to earn 40.8 percent of all professional degrees (National Center for Education Statistics 1994), and by 2005 more women than men are projected to earn doctorates.

Despite this shinny veneer, a closer look at the doctoral fields in which women are enrolled cause concern. Ransom (1990) found that although the percent of doctorates earned by women increased from 21.3 percent in the ten years between 1974 and 1985, during this same time period, segregation of disciplines by sex increased (Ransom 1990). The percent of doctorates earned by men in the fields of engineering (90.4 percent), computer and information sciences (86.7 percent), business (76.7 percent), mathematics (78.6 percent), physical sciences (78.1 percent) and architecture (70.5 percent) confirm that men continue to dominate these fields (1991-1992 data; National Center for Education Statistics 1994).

Access to these academic domains leads to visibly different occupational and financial outcomes. Yet, for women, entry into these traditionally male disciplines has been truncated by their educational experience (Sadker and Sadker 1995).

Institutional Policies and Practices

Hiring and Promotion

Any observations of the hiring structure within universities does nothing to challenge the belief that segregation by sex along lines of prestige, opportunity, and financial outcome is not the natural order. Female faculty earnings are about 80 percent of the salary of their male counterparts (Sax et al., 1996). Female faculty are *inversely* represented in prestigious ranks and institutions; the higher the rank and the more prestigious the institution the fewer female faculty (Dziech and Weiner 1990; Freeman 1997; Sadker and Sadker 1995). At 4-year institutions, 43.5 percent of male faculty are full professors, only 17.3 percent of female faculty hold this rank. Female faculty are over-represented in the lower ranks: 18.4 percent are lecturers/instructors and 37.2 percent are assistant professors compared to 5.76 percent and 22.1 percent, respectively, for male faculty (Sax et al., 1996). Female faculty comprise about 46 percent of the faculty at less prestigious 2-year institutions (Sax et al., 1996). At elite institutions, only 10 to 13 percent of the faculty are women (Freeman 1997; Sadker and Sadker 1995.

Male faculty outnumber female faculty in almost every academic discipline, but segregation by sex within disciplines occurs. Men comprise 98 percent of the faculty in engineering, 83 percent in natural sciences, and 78 percent in social sciences. In the field of education, which has more female than male students, the majority of faculty are male, although women have made gains in this "feminine" discipline and will soon outnumber their male counterparts (1987 data; National Center for Education Statistics 1994).

Policies and Practices

Female faculty lack status and power: they hold lower ranks, are clustered in the "feminine" disciplines, and earn less money even when they hold the same rank as male faculty. They are absent in great numbers from administrative positions. This lack of status and power effects the personal and professional lives of female faculty who are unable to change policies that put them at a disadvantage.

Higher education is not a model for gender equitable policies. The culture of academia results in different professional and personal consequences for its female and male members. Research suggests that for female and male faculty, marriage and children may be differentially related to professional success. Freeman (1977) found that female faculty at elite institutions, compared to their male counterparts, were less likely to be married and to have fewer children if married (Freeman 1977). Recent national data revealed that female faculty are more likely than their male counterparts to report feeling "extreme stress" (44 versus 27 percent) due to factors such as time pressures, household responsibilities, lack of personal time, teaching load, and subtle discrimination(Sax et al., 1996).

Policies and practices that place female faculty at a disadvantage include dual-career marriages and parental leave (Norrell and Norrell 1996). Women tend to marry men equal in professional status (Sax et al., 1996), but for women in higher education, those in dual academic-career marriages suffer consequences. Female spouses are disproportionately represented in the ranks of part-time and temporary teaching positions or are often seen as "add-ons" when both members hold tenure-track positions at the same institution. Although having a profound effect on the professional aspirations of female academicians, institutions of higher education have avoided taking a position of advocacy on this problem.

Similarly, the academy has done little to advocate parental policies that would benefit female faculty. Female faculty who take maternity leave are expected to maintain the same research and service agenda; few institutions make any adjustment in the tenure time-line for women who have taken time out for childbearing (Norrell and Norrell 1996). Yet, for many female faculty the start of her career (i.e., as an untenured assistant professor) and her childbearing years occur simultaneously.

Campus Climate

Sexual Harassment and Rape

Many factors combine to form a chilly campus climate for women. Sexual harassment is one contributor to this climate. Sexual harassment includes sexist jokes in the classroom, unwanted sexual attention, and bribes/threats for grades or academic support (quid pro quo). Most victims of sexual harassment on campus are female. Both female faculty and female students share this experience.

The few available studies on the sexual harassment of female faculty estimate that 20 percent to 50 percent experience some form of sexual harassment, ranging from a hostile work environment to quid pro quo (Fitzgerald 1996; Sandler and Shoop 1997). Although the majority of harassers are male colleagues, female faculty also report harassment by male students.

The lack of status and power held by female faculty, noted in the discussion above, affects their willingness and ability to act as advocates on the problem of sexual harassment (Dziech and Weiner 1990). Given their tentative acceptance into a male dominated academic world, female faculty are under pressure to "join the club", to maintain silence about inequities, to be "colleagues first and women second" (Dziech and Weiner 1990: 56). Only about 22 percent of female faculty who acknowledge incidents of sexual harassment make a formal report (Seals 1997). Female faculty fear reprisals if they speak out, and research supports that many of these fears are legitimate (Fitzgerald 1996). As a consequence of action, they suffer isolation and accusations from colleagues who doubt the veracity of their perceptions (Dziech and Wiener 1990; Galland and Cross 1993, Seals 1997). Female faculty who challenge the silent agreement carefully constructed by male peers, challenge the individuals who have power over their professional status.

Survey data from campuses nationwide suggest that the number of female students who experience some form of sexual harassment ranges from 20 percent to 50 percent (Fitzgerald 1996; Sandler and Shoop 1997; Truax 1996). A recent large-scale study reported numbers as large as 76 percent (Fitzgerald 1996). Of students who experience sexual harassment, about 5 percent to 8 percent experience severe harassment (Truax 1996). Overall, only a small number (3 percent to 5 percent) of students who experience some form of sexual harassment report the incident (Fitzgerald 1996; Sandler and Shoop 1997). Most student fail to report sexual harassment due to fear of reprisals, fear of further harassment or with the sense that authorities would not act. The position faced by female students who are sexually harassed is precarious. Faculty are in positions of power; they exert control over grades, research opportunities, and academic careers.

The real life impact of sexual harassment is high. Frequently, victims of harassment reported disbelief, feelings of guilt, and selfreproachment and they cope by denying, minimizing or avoiding the harasser (Dziech and Weiner, 1990). One study found that 20 percent of female respondents avoided sexual harassment by not enrolling for a course; 5 percent reported dropping a course to avoid harassment (Fitzgerald 1996).

A measure an institution's commitment to eliminating sexism is its willingness to provide a climate safe from discrimination and harassment. Female students face violence in the form of sexual harassment. They also face violence as victims of rape or attempted rape. Most occurrences involve fellow students and often rape occurs within the domain of the fraternity culture (Hirsch 1997). Many institutions maintain silence on this problem.

In a survey of 3,187 college women, Koss found that 84 percent of rape or attempted rape incidents involved someone known to the woman; 57 percent of the rapes occurred on dates (Koss and Harvey 1994). Only 5 percent of the women in the survey reported the rape or attempted rape to authorities. Surveys findings on the number of rape victims vary from 1 in 4 to 1 in 20 (see discussions in Koss and Harvey 1994; Schreiber 1994). The crime of rape on campus appears prevalent but silent; only 387 incidents of forcible rape on universities and colleges were reported in the 1995 Uniform Crime Report (U.S. Department of Justice), a number inconsistent with the survey findings noted above. Perhaps, as Kathleen Hirsch suggested, rape occurs at about the same frequency on campus as it does in the general public. However, campus administrative judicial boards "...largely succeed in creating the impression that crimes against women are aberrations in otherwise civilized communities devoted to the refinement of the mind" (1997: 281).

Discrimination and Inequity in the Classroom

Women enter higher education socialized to acquiesce rather than challenge harassers. They arrive socialized by an educational system that taught them to doubt their ability and compromise their aspirations. Research data reveal that young girls suffer a decline in self esteem and self-confidence beginning in childhood. By the time they enter college, many doubt their ability to succeed (AAUW 1992; Pascarella et al., 1997; Sadker and Sadker 1995). The American Association of University Women, in *How Schools Shortchange Girls*, report "compelling evidence that girls are not receiving the same quality, or even quantity, of education as their brothers" (AAUW 1992: v).

Sexism in higher education occurs in the overt and covert messages communicated to young women. Disparity in academic positions of male and female faculty sustains the belief that women have less to offer. Sexism also exists in the differential esteem accorded to the achievements and performances of men. How can a college woman not recognize that her endeavors are not highly valued? As Chamberlain (1991) noted, the findings of numerous studies show that both men and women rank achievements attributed to men higher than the same achievements attributed to women.

On college campuses, sexism extends to the classroom. Male students dominate classroom conversations, they talk longer, more frequently, and make more interruptions. College faculty who provide male students with more attention, eye contact, and wait time for answers perpetuate women's second class status in academia (Sadker and Sadker 1995). What is the cumulative effect of the chilly campus climate on female students? Data suggest that the climate can negatively influence cognitive development, especially for female students in 2-year institutions (Pascarella et al., 1997).

The Role of Faculty

Higher education involves the indirect transmission of values and beliefs and individual faculty members are the transmitters. The words and actions of faculty carry meaning. They convey to students judgments and expectations about their ability, worth, and potential place in society. By exhibiting prejudicial and discriminatory attitudes and behaviors, faculty perpetuate the status quo. By demonstrating equity in their thinking and actions, faculty invite students to do the same. However, surveys of students and alumni yield reports of prejudicial statements and behaviors by faculty.

Inequity continues to plague the academy despite gains in enrollment and visibility that have been made by female, minority, gay and lesbian, and lower socio-economic groups. For the authors, this conviction has been bolstered by findings from studies that assessed two of the major determinants of campus cultural climate: faculty and institutional support (Miller and Miller 1997; Miller et al., 1997; 1998; Schroth et al., 1997; 1998).

The targets of five regional, state, and national surveys were faculty and programs in the field of education.[1] Data on faculty attitudes and behaviors regarding race, gender, sexual preference, and social class were gathered by one of two methods: (a) anonymous surveys mailed to faculty who self-reported attitudes and behaviors, or (b) surveys and interviews of graduates regarding perceptions of faculty attitudes and behaviors. Additionally, faculty and graduates were asked to report their perceptions of programmatic and institutional support for culture-fair policies and practices.

Findings were remarkably consistent across the five studies. In general, both faculty and graduates perceived greater institutional bias than individual bias (except graduates who reported greater bias in faculty behaviors about homosexuality). In general, faculty behaviors were rated as more biased than their attitudes. This trend, with one exception, was found in studies that surveyed faculty directly and in studies that asked graduates to report perceptions of faculty.

The most notable finding was that heterosexism emerged as a dominant theme. Overwhelmingly, faculty and institutional bias based on sexual orientation was greater than bias based on class, gender, or race. This finding is in accord with other studies that have found higher discrimination based on sexual orientation than based on gender or race (Wells and Daly 1992).

Although quantifying and labeling "degree of bias" is a difficult task, faculty and institutional bias generally fell in a low-moderate to moderate range. The Survey of Cultural Attitudes and Behaviors (Miller and Miller 1997) was used in these five studies. Subjects responded to questions using a 7-point scale where higher scores indicate greater bias. Averaged scores of graduates' perceptions of faculty bias ranged from 2.6 on the racism scale (attitudes) to 4.5 on the heterosexism scale (behaviors). Graduates' perceptions of programmatic and institutional bias ranged from 3.1 (racism) to 4.3 (heterosexism). However, faculty rated their own biases (and those of the institution) lower than did the graduates in the studies noted above. Averaged faculty self-reported scores ranged from 2.1 on the racism scale (attitudes) to 3.2 on the heterosexism scale (behaviors). Faculty perceptions of program and institutional bias ranged from 2.9 (racism) to 3.8 (heterosexism). .

None of the studies revealed that sexism was identified as the most prevalent "ism". However, the discrepancy between faculty self-perceptions (1.8, attitudes; 2.3, behaviors) and the perceptions that graduates held about their faculty (3.0, faculty attitudes; 3.1, faculty behaviors) reveal one dimension of the gender equity problem on college campuses.

Despite the fact that faculty rated themselves, and their institutions, less harshly than did graduates, the studies yielded remarkably consistent findings.   This consistency is more alarming given that participants in these studies were drawn from the field of education, an academic area where emphasis on diversity equals or exceeds that found in other disciplines.   Professional standards, legislative mandates, and social norms require that elementary and secondary teachers, counselors, and administrators demonstrate a range of cultural knowledge and competencies.   Consequently, education preparation programs are mandated to offer multicultural education courses. Faculty in these programs are expected to educate accordingly.   These are strong reasons to expect considerably lower findings of bias in the studies that we conducted.

Faculty exemplify the knowledge and values of the academy.   Their attitudes and beliefs about women, as well as about other cultural groups (i.e., minority, gay and lesbian, and lower-income students) carry powerful messages about who is included and who is expected to succeed.   This power is also communicated within the community of scholars. Academicians who investigate their profession can expect to be marginalized and discounted or face the antagonistic reactions of colleagues.   Reporting their research on sexual harassment, Dziech and Weiner (1990) observed "Some academics seem threatened, angry, and hostile to those who ask questions about it (sexual harassment)". They recounted these angry responses, concluding "Each of us has about thirty more years to work with some of these people, and lately that seems like a very long time.   There are days when we doubt that our profession will muster the objectivity and courage to make hard decisions about it own members....." (p. 6). Is there any wonder that few academicians choose to investigate their own profession?

Ample evidence suggests that gender inequities exist in higher education. Faculty must realize that they are key to transforming this culture.   They must be willing to use their ability to understand complex issues and engage in objective and scientific inquiry to understand their role in perpetuating inequity. They must be willing to use their hearts to choose to change.

Model for Creating a Gender-fair Academy

The model described in this section is designed to produce the following outcomes in postsecondary institutions: (a) gender-competent administrators, faculty, and staff, (b) gender-fair institutional policies, practices, and standards, (c) gender-fair academic programs, curricular materials, and teaching practices, and (d) ongoing commitments to gender-fair policies and practices. Adapted from the work of Sue and Sue (1990), this model was originally developed for training culturally competent counselors. However, its elegance and relevance qualify it as a useful approach for gender training in larger institutional settings. For purposes of brevity, "faculty" will be used to refer to university and college administrators and faculty.

This model is comprised of three stages that include: (a) developing personal awareness, (b) acquiring knowledge and understanding of gender issues, and (c) implementing gender-sensitive interventions.

Stage I: Developing Personal Awareness

Sue and Sue (1990) identified five characteristics of people who have developed personal awareness of cultural (including gender) dynamics that affect their beliefs, attitudes, values, feelings, and behaviors. These characteristics include: (a) moving from a position of cultural unawareness to one of awareness and sensitivity to their own cultural heritage and to valuing and respecting cultural (including gender) differences, (b) developing awareness of their own values and biases and how they affect persons of the opposite sex with whom they interact, (c) developing comfort with differences that exist between themselves and persons of the opposite sex in terms of attitudes, beliefs, values, etc., (d) developing sensitivity to circumstances (e.g., personal biases, inability to understand another person because of gender differences) that may indicate a need to refer a person of the opposite sex to another professional for services, and (e) acknowledging sexist attitudes, beliefs, and feelings.

Some faculty may perceive the processes required to achieve this level of personal awareness to be so complex, challenging, and threatening as to be impractical. Such perceptions may explain the lack of substantive gender training opportunities for faculty on many of our nation's campuses.   They may also help to explain the reluctance of faculty to enthusiastically participate in gender training opportunities when they are offered.   Nevertheless, personal awareness is a critical dimension of all personal, institutional, and social change processes.   Consequently, if the academy is to realize its potential as a gender-fair educational and work climate, a functional process to generate personal awareness must be identified and implemented.

Stage II: Acquiring Knowledge and Understanding of Gender Issues

A major goal of this stage is to help faculty gain sufficient knowledge about their own and opposite sex dynamics and issues to facilitate acceptance of different worldviews in a nonjudgmental manner.   In acquiring gender knowledge, each faculty engages in a process of gender role-taking.   This type of learning requires that faculty adopt the perspective of a member of the opposite sex in order to learn about the group's background as well as the hopes, fears, and daily living experiences of its members.   By engaging in this process, faculty come to understand not only gender dynamics, but also the wider sociopolitical system with which members of the opposite sex struggle in their daily lives (Sue and Sue 1990).

Three criteria mark the successful completion of this stage. Knowledgeable faculty will: (a) possess specific knowledge about gender dynamics and issues of their own and opposite sex groups, (b) understand how the U.S. sociopolitical system operates in with respect to its treatment of their own and opposite sex groups, and (c) demonstrate knowledge of institutional barriers that inhibit or prevent their own and opposite sex groups from fully using the services of the institution (Sue and Sue 1990).

In order to meet these criteria, faculty must first be provided with specific information about persons of opposite sex represented by students and faculty on their campus.   This information must include a history of the opposite sex group and enculturation experiences.   It must also include facts about world views, beliefs, attitudes, values, time orientation, relationship to nature, preferred type of relationships with other people, mode of activity (i.e., doing vs. being), norms, customs, and traditions of the group.   Successful participation in such experiences requires the leadership of a gender expert in facilitating small group activities.

Additionally, faculty must receive accurate information regarding the historical and current treatment of opposite sex groups by the United States government and social institutions. Histories of abuse, neglect, oppression, and other forms of sexual and gender discrimination must be provided if faculty are to develop a genuine understanding of the group's dynamics in a larger social context. In addition, social, political, and economic consequences of sexual/gender bias and discrimination must be examined if lasting insights are to be gained.

Finally, faculty must be provided with factual information regarding the roles that colleges and universities have played in perpetuating gender bias and discrimination. Only with such knowledge can faculty develop an understanding of opposite sex group members' belief systems, values, and behaviors.

Stage III: Implementing Gender-sensitive Interventions

Having gained greater awareness and understanding of gender issues and dynamics, it remains for faculty to put this newfound information into practice. Three intervention skills that reflect sensitivity to the needs of opposite sex students and faculty include: (a) demonstrating an ability to send and receive both verbal and nonverbal communications accurately and appropriately with members of the opposite sex, (b) exercising institutional intervention skills when appropriate, and, (c) recognizing the limitations of one's own gender competence and taking appropriate action (Sue and Sue 1990).

To communicate effectively with opposite sex students and faculty requires practice in the use of communication skills and styles that may be significantly different from those commonly used by members of one's own sex. Language use among men and women is characterized by nuances that may not be immediately discernable to the uninitiated. In addition, nonverbal communications take on quite different meanings for men and women. Not only must faculty understand these dynamics and be able to accurately interpret linguistic and nonlinguistic cues, they must also learn to send communications in the idiom of the other sex.

Gender-skilled faculty understand institutional dynamics that have limited access to colleges and universities, promoted discriminatory policies and practices, and created educational inequities. Armed with knowledge of structural prejudice and its consequences, faculty are positioned to offer institutional intervention skills on behalf of opposite sex students and faculty when appropriate.   These interventions frequently occur outside the comfort of one's office and may require faculty to assume the roles of consultant, ombudsman, outreach person, or facilitator of indigenous support systems (Sue and Sue 1990).   Such forms of assistance are offered with the understanding that barriers experienced by persons of the opposite sex are frequently rooted in institutional dynamics, and therefore require institutional interventions.

Understanding that no one can effectively communicate with, relate to, and assist all people, competent faculty recognize their personal limitations.   When gender issues arise that limit their effectiveness, gender-competent faculty anticipate how these problems will affect others   and   openly   communicate   their   limitations.   Such acknowledgements   are   intended   to   communicate   honesty, understanding, and a desire to be of assistance to opposite sex students or faculty, despite one's limitations.   In such cases, faculty may seek consultation or refer the individual to a more competent colleague.

Implementing the Model in a College or University Setting

Executing the model described above is a difficult task.   It requires faculty to reflect upon and reveal private beliefs, attitudes, and values. It further requires faculty to examine the possible gender-biased attitudes or discriminatory behaviors.   The obvious threats associated with such tasks require that training be provided by gender experts who structure workshops to insure the psychological and personal safety of all participants. Group members must be carefully selected to eliminate the possibility of personal or political repercussions when sensitive information is disclosed.   To achieve this goal, facilitators must develop written contracts with all participants to maintain the confidentiality of group communications.

Training should occur in small groups comprised of no more than 10 faculty in order to maximize participation by all group members. Sessions should be conducted for a period of 90 to 120 minutes in order to insure adequate time for exploration, yet not exceed the limits of attention or comfort.   The number of training sessions per stage should be determined by need.   However, no more than three sessions per stage should be offered in order to accommodate faculty schedules and university budgets.   Only in an environment that provides for the safety, comfort, and well being of all participants can productive explorations occur that lead to deeper personal awareness.

The experience of gaining insight into personal gender attitudes, beliefs, and behaviors (Stage I), may help participants to understand the importance of enhancing gender knowledge (Stage II) and building gender competence (Stage III). Because faculty will exhibit varying levels of insight, it is recommended that group leaders evaluate these levels at the conclusion of the Stage I workshop. Doing so will facilitate the selection of appropriate faculty for Stage II workshops. This process should be repeated at the end of Stage II workshops. As was the case in the first stage, group leaders for Stage II and Stage III workshops must carefully select participants in order to insure their psychological safety and to prevent any possible retaliation for views expressed. As participants develop knowledge and skills, opportunities for practice in realistic campus scenarios should be provided.

For example, group leaders should facilitate discussions of how faculty can apply newly acquired competencies in their professional roles. Participants may be asked to engage in 20-minute dialogues on topics that include:

- What are the beliefs values, philosophies, and mission statements that drive this institution, and do they contain any conceivable hint of gender insensitivity, bias, or discrimination?
- Do institutional policies and practices derived from the above beliefs, values, and philosophies reflect any form of gender bias or discrimination?
- Are institutional standards interpreted, applied, and enforced equally for all students, faculty, and staff, regardless of their sex?
- Do academic programs recruit, welcome, and retain both female and male faculty and students?
- Are faculty sensitive to the gender needs of students and are they competent to provide gender-fair instruction?
- Have curricular materials in every department been evaluated to identify gender stereotyping or bias?
- What are the responsibilities of administrators, faculty, and staff to enhance the gender competence of the students?
- What are the responsibilities of administrators, faculty, and staff to resolve problems in any of the areas identified above?

To implement all three stages of this model requires enormous commitments of time, money and other valuable resources. All faculty must commit to attend between three and nine workshops, each of which lasts from 90 to 120 minutes. This sequence requires a total time commitment of between 4.5-18 hours per faculty. As noted above, the expertise required to conduct this type of training is considerable. Not only must trainers possess gender expertise, but they must also be highly skilled small group facilitators. In addition to what may appear to be formidable demands on faculty time and university budgets, faculty resistance to participation in such training may be a major obstacle. Many faculty will undoubtedly question the need for or value of such training.

Despite these constraints, problems, and protestations, administrators must carefully consider the extent to which they should go to insure gender competence on their campuses. Questions that may guide these considerations should include, "What are the alternatives to substantive gender training for faculty and students?" and "What are the consequences and costs to the academy, faculty, students, and society if substantive gender training is not offered?"

Summary and Conclusions

As noted throughout this chapter, U.S. colleges and universities fall far short of systematically embodying the democratic principles of equality and "justice for all" in their policies and practices. Inequities in power, salary, rank, and access based on sex continue to dominate the academic landscape. Sexism is a pervasive and seemingly unyielding feature of campus life. These conditions persist despite: (a) more than thirty years of federal and state legislation designed to eliminate sex bias and discrimination, (b) the rise of a national women's movement that has worked to create awareness, understanding, and greater respect for the contributions of women in American society, and (c) more than a decade of cultural and gender training opportunities for administrators and faculty on our nation's campuses.

Campus administrators and faculty can choose to examine personal beliefs, attitudes, and values for evidence of gender bias and discrimination. They can further choose to evaluate institutional mission statements, philosophies, and policies in light of the same concerns. They can elect to examine program content and curricular materials to insure gender relevant and sensitive offerings. And they can train students to understand, respect, and accept gender differences; critical life skills for the twenty-first century.

Whether colleges and universities will guide future generations to a deeper understanding of and respect for gender differences or acquiesce to powerful forces that maintain gender inequities is a question that can be answered. The answer lies in the personal will of those with the power and responsibility to shape the future: the Academy's administrators and faculty.

Notes

1. The authors wish to acknowledge Texas A&M University-Commerce for funding four of the five surveys described in this section.

Chapter 4

Social Systems Barriers of Women in Academia: A Review of Historical and Current Issues

Donna Arlton, Ara Lewellen, and Barbara Grissett

Why do some women college graduates earn one-third less than men with comparable educational backgrounds? Why are women faculty primarily concentrated in low-ranked, non-tenured positions? Why are women deans, vice-presidents, and presidents at major teaching institutions a rare occurrence?

The purpose of this chapter is to examine the psychological and social barriers affecting women facultys' promotions, rank, and salaries in the 1990's. There are a proliferation of national and state level quantitative analyses that provide descriptive statistics of female faculty by academic year, rank, salary, and public versus private institutional type. For example, the National Education Association reported the latest statistics nationwide on sex distribution of faculty in higher education and numerous short reports on topics such as faculty workload disparities by sex and ethnicity. The National Association for Women in Education is a quarterly publication about women's issues on campuses nationwide (Sandler 1997). State and state institutions also provide data regarding women faculty such as Texas A&M University's recent study for the Texas Legislature on women and minority faculty and professional staff (Ashworth and James 1997). However, few reports provide qualitative analyses that can be used to implement social changes. This chapter discusses the paradox of women's superior achievements in academia versus their limited rewards in promotions, rank, and salaries. The method of analysis is a social systems perspective that simultaneously holds women responsible for their growth and achievements while at the same time recognizing the impact of social conditions that limit women's opportunities for equity. Social conditions may be defined as the cultural environment that includes historical forces, kin and non-kin groups, organizations, and communities extending nationally and internationally (Chetkow-Yanoov 1992). The authors suggest that the following social conditions continue to influence opportunities for women faculty and administrators on college campuses:

1. Historical socio-cultural forces, including economic conditions, social sanctions, and biased methods of evaluation of women's capabilities
2. Kin and non-kin group expectations of women's roles as child-bearers and primary child-care givers
3. Institutional biases affecting evaluation of performance and resulting reward system
4. Family, institutional and community career tracking of women into specific degree programs limiting future opportunities
5. Career ladders which favor male dominated disciplines.

The authors present women's progress through the 1990's and make recommendations for increasing equal rewards for separate but equal accomplishments of women in academia.

A Social Systems Perspective of Women's Progress in Higher Education

Social systems' scholars search for ways to view issues and problems through the interplay of persons with their environments (Germain 1973; Engel 1980; Coulton 1981). They are cautious about easy answers that seek to explain problems without looking at the broad cultural context of events, time, place, available information and ideas. Social system frameworks for understanding social problems focus on environmental complexity with multiple causes operating simultaneously. What are some of the environmental complexities of women's past and present achievements in academia? A brief historical overview begins with looking at socio-cultural expectations of women in the United States in the 18th and 19th centuries through the present.

Historical socio-cultural forces affecting women's appropriate roles

Since their entry on college campuses 150 years ago, women's participation on college campuses have been mediated by socio-cultural sanctions of their appropriate roles. Women's roles as students, faculty, and administrators were sanctioned when men were unavailable to fill these roles. As a reserve force they filled positions when men were needed elsewhere, such as on the farm or at the battlefronts. Declining enrollment by men following the Civil War sparked several state universities to consider admitting women. Social opposition was partially offset because women continued to perform domestic chores at home and on campus (Chamberlain 1988).

The women's movement gave women the psychological tools to envision themselves as capable of attaining a college education, particularly to pursue degrees in the fields of teaching, nursing, and social work. These were professions where women could use skills in which they were already skilled at home and in communities. Society sanctioned these roles which were needed to rebuild the country with cheap labor. Women taught for one-half less or less of men's salaries for the same job (Woody 1966, original edition 1929). But widespread beliefs about women's biological and reproductive health promoted the idea that women could not and should not participate in the workforce in the same roles as men (Chamberlain 1988). Consequently, few women were in educational programs outside of human services and rarely did they hold leadership positions on campuses.

Chamberlain suggests that women as faculty were not taken seriously. She asserts that rational processes have not been used to evaluate women's contributions from the beginning of women's roles as faculty. No single trend can account for this phenomenon but cultural tradition appears to have played a strong role. The tradition of universities outside of America was to blend church and education so that students were members of clerical orders as well as scholars. Women were excluded from being members of clerical orders. Thus the church and its view of appropriate women's roles may have added to the social ideas of the time that women were not suited as scholars.

Ironically, conversely, the church may have led the way for women in educational administration although not until the recent decades of this century. The majority of women college presidents in this country through the 1970's were nuns. The connotation of nuns as other than active sexual, reproductive women may have played a role in opening doors for women. From the 1970's through 1981, women's representation overall in university administration increased 13.8 percent, far and above the 4.6 percent increase in women faculty representation (Frances and Mensel 1981).

The trend to advance women as deans, vice-presidents, and presidents has come about only recently. There is some evidence that this may be a reduction in Americans' discrimination and prejudice against women in leadership roles (Chamberlain 1992). Other social systems such as industrial and service organizations in the United States also reflect similar reductions in actions designed to prevent women from full participation. Of particular interest is the new profile of women executives in the United States: they are middle-aged (44 years – mean), married, and have spouses who are also employed outside the home (Korn/Ferry and UCLA Anderson 1992). The taboo against women as both sexual beings and business leaders may be declining.

A decline in prejudice against women's biological sex may have been simply because of new energy and information. Systems's thinker Checkland (1981) suggests that some new attitudes are the result of enormous amounts of new technology and information. Special programs established in the 1970's to promote women in administrative careers seem to have resulted from efforts of men like Alan Pifer of the Carnegie Corporation who believed that the time had come to document and change inequalities in women's participation in college leadership. Affirmative actions programs were also forcing government and business leaders to establish more money and positions for women in leadership positions in academia. However, by the mid 1980's in a follow-up survey of the first national survey on salary levels of women and minorities in higher education, Frances and Mensel (1981) revealed that women held only 20 percent of all administrative positions in colleges and earned less than men in every position. Further, women administrators through the 1980's were still primarily working in non-chief executive positions, such as director of library services, director of student affairs, director of student placement, etc..

Prigogine and Stengers (1984) also argue that crises affect social change because they force decisions that can no longer be ignored. The drive for equity for women as students, faculty, and administrators undoubtedly benefited from the pressures of the 1960's and 1970's and the resulting new federal laws, government grants, loans, and affirmative action programs. Women as students could apply for loans without discrimination of biological sex. Women s faculty fell under the Title VII of the Civil Rights Act which was enacted in 1972 prohibiting discrimination in hiring at all educational institutions. Also enacted in 1972, Executive Orders to ensure equal opportunities for desirable jobs benefited women seeking administrative roles in academia.

Lastly, Taylor (1975) points out that great leaders affect great changes. Many outstanding leaders from disparate sectors of society converged in the 1970's to espouse equity for women. Social leaders of the women's movement, politicians, trustees of colleges and universities, and corporate leaders enacted new strategies for the advancement of women. One organization of women, Higher Education Resources Services (HERS) under the leadership of Sheila Tobias, Associate Provost of Wesleyan University, established a resource network and central registry to nominate qualified women for high level academic positions (Horning 1978).

This brief historical overview of converging social system events and social changes reveal how women in academia have moved from no representation on college campuses 150 years ago to multiple roles and achievements in the last decades of the 20th century. Some of the conditions leading to social change for women in higher education have been changes in economic conditions, new sanctions of appropriate women's roles, changes in technology and information, social crises, and new leaders. However, many historical socio-cultural issues reappear in the 1990's as barriers to women's equal opportunities on campus. For example, the most highly sanctioned roles for women are still those of child-bearers and primary child-care givers. Women returning to school who do not have support systems to help them replace child-caring and other home roles are stigmatized more severely than other returning students (Breese and O'Toole 1995). The time spent at home affects when women enter academic programs and the length of time they spend obtaining degrees. The next sections examine current social systems barriers that contribute to a paradox of under-rewarded achievements for women as students, faculty, and administrators.

Kin and Non-Kin Group Expectations for Women's Roles

A longitudinal study of educational achievements in higher education by the US Department of Education revealed the following paradox of expectations for women's academic achievements whereby women's high school academic performance was far superior to that of men. In terms of national measures of general learned abilities, the impact of women's course of study in high school—particularly in math and science—was equivalent to that of men.

At the same time, their educational aspirations were lower than those of men, an attitude influenced, no doubt, by their parents' lower educational aspirations for daughters than for sons. Nonetheless, they continued their education at the same rate as men, were rewarded more with scholarships for post-secondary education, and completed degrees (associate and bachelor's) at a faster pace than men (Adelman 1992). Women students in the 1990's continue high educational achievements but salary equity remains far behind rewards for men (Knopp 1996). What social system expectations perpetuate this paradox of rewards?

Women as child-bearers and primary child-care givers take longer to complete advanced degrees than men because of family responsibilities and the financial burden of education (Barkhymer and Dorsett 1991). The extra time to complete their degrees results in less work experience than men. Further, women's work experience at home is discounted by employers who view work at home as "no work experience". Collectively, these social conditions contribute to lower salaries for women in comparable positions. In 1991, degreed women in full-time jobs earned about one-third less than men (Ottinger and Sikula 1993). Ottinger and Sikula reported that men and women's salary differentials were accounted for primarily by child-caring and the associated loss of years of job experience.

Other important variables in salary differentials were occupation, industry, type of employer, highest degree, college major, and amount of mathematics earned (Ottinger and Sikula 1993). Women are employed predominately in health-related fields and teaching where salaries have traditionally trailed other professions such as business, math, and law. For graduates in the 1990's, these conditions may be changing; women are moving into fields of law, medicine, veterinary medicine, and pharmacy and they are completing advanced degrees at or above the rate of men (Knopp 1996). Despite motherhood and career tracking into traditional fields, women received 55 percent of all degrees earned in 1992-93. Respectively, they earned 40 percent of all bachelor's degrees, 50 percent of all master's degrees, and 50 percent of all doctoral degrees (Knopp 1996).

Women's largest social barrier to continuing progress in academic achievements may be the age-old choice of career or family. In a recent survey of first year male students from 427 colleges and universities, the majority agreed with the statement, "Married women's activities are best confined to home and family" (Higher Education Research Institute 1993). It appears that women have made tremendous strides in the role of student but future progress continues to be impeded by socio-cultural conceptions of appropriate women's roles and by women's career choices in traditionally low-paying professions.

What about women whose jobs are on college campuses? The next section examines barriers to equitable reward systems for women faculty, particularly barriers to salary equity and tenure and promotion.

Institutional Bias

Recent reports suggest that current women faculty have remained in low-ranked, non-tenured positions of instructors and lecturers. Over 40 percent are part-time and 50 percent working in lecturer positions (Knopp 1996). Some progress has been made with women moving into assistant and associate professor positions, but few reach the rank of full professor. Less than half of the women faculty have tenure compared to 78 percent of men. Salary differentials between men and women across all ranks has broadened, not lessened (Sandler 1997).

In a recent report by the Higher Education Research Institute (HERI 1997), 34,000 professors were surveyed. Findings revealed that many differences remain between men and women on the issue of goal attainments versus rewards. With rank held constant, women earned 12 percent less than men although only 10 percent of men versus 30 percent of women believed that salary differentials were due to discrimination. Family issues interrupted 28 percent of women's faculty careers compared with 5 percent of men's faculty careers.

Rewards for female faculty are slow in coming. This is mainly due to institutional biases that continue salary gaps between male and female faculty, disproportionate heavy teaching loads of female faculty, problems of female faculty in receiving fair tenure evaluations, and inhospitable climates that provide female faculty with less information and resources than their male counterparts.

Career Tracking In to Traditional Female Professions

According to data gathered by the College and University Personnel Association (CUPA 1997), women administrators are more likely to be found in student affairs and external affairs than in academic and administrators' affairs. In all of these areas, women are greatly outnumbered by men. On average, they hold 27 percent of academic deanships. This ranges from 97 percent deans of nursing to 8 percent deans of law. At lower levels of an organization, the proportion of women increases. For example, women currently hold 28 percent of positions for director of admissions, 50 percent for associate director, and 66 percent for assistant director.

In 1994-95, women have increased overall administrative positions but many reward systems remain elusive. Many more women are chief executives in colleges and universities yet women earn as much as 12 percent less than men in the same positions. And the majority of women's administrative positions are still concentrated in student and external affairs.

Clearly, reward systems of women administrators in academia remain sex related. Warner and De Fleur (1993) identify several factors contributing to this situation including: 1) personal characteristics; 2) career paths; and 3) networks and mentoring. Women are disadvantaged by employment records reflecting less prestigious jobs and resources, less advanced degrees, and less willingness to relocate geographically. Their careers are likely in the arts, humanities, or education; whereas, most college presidents, vice-presidents, and provosts come from liberal arts backgrounds.

It is the norm for academic administrators to have significant experience in faculty roles. Faculty experience is the principal entry point for administrative futures. However, the process of matching candidates to jobs are carried out through faculty based search committees composed primarily of men. Even though a wide range of candidates is sought, the outcome is usually the selection of an individual with whom the committee members feel the most comfortable with and who they perceive will fit in with the community.

Discussion and Summary

The increased representation of women students, faculty, and administrators on college and university campuses has not been followed by equitable rewards for their accomplishments. Comparing historical and current trends, many social barriers which women appeared to have conquered in the past have reappeared in the 1990's. For example, two major barriers to women's progress continue to be the stigma associated with roles outside the home and family and career tracking into traditional women's fields. This, in turn, affects timing of entering college, the field of study chosen, loss of work experience, and resulting lower salaries.

For women faculty, family issues affect timing of careers. Another major social barrier is the non-rational process of evaluating women's capabilities. Women faculty are often expected to carry heavier service workloads then men yet these duties are not taken into consideration when promotions are sought. In addition, student evaluations of women faculty carry many negative social biases yet often these evaluations may affect opportunities for promotion and tenure. Further, the process of promotion and tenure in many colleges and universities is still secretive making due process impossible to evaluate.

Recommendations

The situation for women in higher education is clearly problematic; however, a social systems perspective suggests that even modest changes in a small number of systems can create major social changes. Suggestions to increase opportunities for women's parity with men in the areas of promotion, rank, and salaries are presented across system levels: kin and non-kin groups, local schools and communities, institutions, and state and federal levels. In presenting our recommendations, we believe that the implementation of these concrete measures can significantly contribute to the creation of a woman-centered university.

We believe that a social systems perspective necessitates a strong commitment from institutional leaders to give women's concerns a voice on campuses from classrooms through administrative bodies. There also needs to be a review of institutional policies and procedures for their effect on gender issues such as performance evaluations, salary equity, and representation in administration. The university needs to develop formal plans for mentoring new women students, faculty, and administrators and strive to provide affordable, quality childcare on campus.

Furthermore, in the area of familial policies, we believe universities should develop an institution-wide concern for children and families with appropriate policies and programs promoting support for parents with primary childcare.   Additionally, performance review standards should be rewritten which are clearly open and fair and universities should promote a healthy, nurturing environment for women through formal and informal support networks.

Lastly, in the area of professional development, universities should ensure that there are opportunities for women to participate in leadership programs such as those offered by the American Council on Education Fellows Program, American Council on Education National Identification Program for the Advancement of Women in Higher Education, Higher Education Resource Services (HERS) and other related programs.   Furthermore, a social system's perspective leading to the creation of a woman-centered university promotes opportunities for women students to meet successful businesswomen from diverse non-traditional women's fields.

Chapter 5

The Empress's New Clothes: Expanding the Boundaries of International Relations Theory and Practice in the Classroom.

JoAnn DiGeorgio-Lutz

International Relations (IR) has generally regarded women and gender related issues as insignificant political actors and topics of world affairs. Women as practitioners of world politics along with gender based themes were simply irrelevant in a field that established its theoretical and practical foundations on the assumptions of the realist paradigm. According to the tenets of realism the state alone is the principal actor in world affairs and its concomitant quest for security remains the dominant issue-area of scholarly importance. Based on this foundation, it is not incomprehensible that the nature and scope of the field did not include an awareness of gender and its relationship to international politics. Even though the boundaries of the field have expanded over the years to accommodate paradigms that include non-state actors as global participants alongside an increased range of issue-areas that warranted academic inquiry, women as practitioners of world affairs and, topics pertaining to gender continued to remain "hidden" from these expanded frontiers.

In part, women remain unseen as practitioners on the world stage because they seldom hold elite positions in the institutions of many governments that are still dominated by men preoccupied with issues of national security. On those rare occasions when women electorally acquired leadership roles, such as that of prime minister, their ascent to power was, and still is, often attributed to their ability to successfully behave according to socially defined constructs of masculine political behavior.[1]

Additionally, women and issues of gender continue to remain an invisible feature of IR because of several factors germane to the field. Despite the entry of women into the field, IR continues to remain overwhelming dominated by males.[2] One of the implications of a male majority is the impact that males continue to exert on the subject matter of the field and the research agenda of scholarly significance. Needless to say these topics still primarily consist of socially constructed notions of masculine international political behavior that emphasize issues relating to international conflict and security. As Peterson and Runyon note "the preponderance of male scholars and practitioners explains in part the silence on gender. . . ." Simply stated, it never occurs to the male majority in the field to relate the substance of gender to international affairs including studies on conflict and security.

As such, the traditionally male-defined subject matter of IR has served to obscure the presence of gender. Topics such as war, national security, economic and foreign policy issues were all thought to be areas beyond the concern, and in some instances, the intellectual capability of women. Aside from the unseen role of women as practitioners of international affairs, the realist version of international relations theory has given scant attention to gender as a legitimate avenue of scholarly inquiry. The tenets of the predominant paradigm of the field continue to preach that security issues are still preeminent and power is a key concept within the hierarchy of international issues. Even though our traditional interpretation of national security linked to military power has given way to economic power as the cornerstone of security in the post-cold war era, the importance of gender in this area is often excluded.[3] Lastly, IR has always been somewhat of an insular field. As such, it is hindered to a certain degree because it remains isolated from other fields of political science that, on the surface, appear to benefit from the growing presence of women.

However, in recent years women scholars within the field of IR have begun to challenge this inherent "gender bias" that continues to neglect the impact of gender and still considers women as unimportant actors in world affairs. According to these scholars, this bias renders a false and incomplete picture of international relations because it underestimates the important role that women do exercise in such areas as international political economy, foreign policy, and international organizations. Moreover, with the demise of the Soviet Union and the end of the Cold War in the late 1980s, the scope of IR has begun to widen considerably. Scholars and practitioners alike are beginning to give increased attention to areas generally defined as "low politics." These areas include peace studies, global migration, human rights, democratization, and environmental politics--areas in which gender is thought to be an important ingredient.[4]

Owing to the persistent efforts of women scholars, many in the field are endeavoring to restructure IR's male-dominated boundaries by redefining its theoretical constructs to include gender as part of theory building in the field. According to Peterson and Runyan, gender analysis is salient both as a "substantive topic" and as a method of analyzing world affairs. According to their guideposts, gender is an important substantive topic because it allows us to examine the field's effects on gender; that is, where and how women are situated in the realm of world politics relative to men. As a method of analysis, gender is salient with respect to the filters, or "lenses" we employ to categorize gender's effects. In this regard we can view the impact of gender itself on the field. Even though the task of re-conceptualizing the field to include gender as a salient feature of mainstream IR remains a monumental challenge, it is not an impossible task. Nor is it the only assignment at hand. Redefining the conceptual boundaries of the field to include gender both as a method of analysis and a legitimate topic of inquiry is only half the battle. The other half requires us to extend our reach into the classroom and consciously include the women and other minorities we teach into the subject matter of our field.

As noted in the introduction, it usually takes a critical mass to bring about institutional change regardless if the institution in question is a university or a departmental field. However, the level of critical mass needed to institute the substantive, methodological, and pedagogical gender-based changes within IR requires us to do more than participate at gender-sponsored panels at leading conferences and adopt gender-oriented textbooks for courses limited to topics on women and politics. It requires us to strive for gender parity in the classroom by actively including the women we teach in the various areas of the field where masculine constructs about world politics still dominate. In doing so we can begin to dispel the social and culturally constructed notions of masculine and feminine that continue to consign women and issues of gender as unimportant features of world affairs. As disciples of institutional change not only do we have an obligation to transform the IR curriculum to include gender as part and parcel of the field's substantive matter, we also must include women and other minorities we instruct in the process of change. By reconstructing the boundaries of what we teach in the proverbial trenches, that is, the classroom, we can begin to compliment the work of IR women scholars who struggle for the inclusion of gender in the field at the conceptual level. In addition, our efforts here could permeate other departments within a university thereby creating a spill-over effect that could eventually reach the needed critical mass for a woman-centered university. Moreover, the need to include women and other minorities in the curriculum carries additional significance for other fields in political science as well as other departments within a university. There appears to be a growing trend across many college campuses to acknowledge, respect, and understand the cultural diversity that characterizes contemporary American society. The depiction of American society as a "melting pot" is anachronistic. Alongside gender and the element of race, American culture reflects a variety of religions, languages, ethnic groups, and economic distinctions that are mirrored in the classroom. As facilitators of learning, I believe that we have an obligation to structure the learning environment in all disciplines to acknowledge and include the diversity of cultures present in our student body.

In laying a foundation for change, this paper serves a dual purpose. On one level it raises awareness of the need to incorporate gender as a salient component of international affairs into IR as a field. On another, it discusses the pedagogic journey that led me to transform my IR curriculum and to actively include the women in the classroom. However, change is never easy. My own experiences at transforming my retinue of IR courses to include gender as pertinent subject matter along with actively including women in the classroom did not occur spontaneously. Instead, it took a more evolutionary course and it required that I go beyond the comfort zone of the discipline's traditional subject matter and explore alternative ways of teaching and learning. It also required that I give serious thought to my teaching goals apart from the more content-oriented objectives that previously dominated my curriculum intentions.

Lecture versus Active Learning

For many IR faculty members, graduate school was not a training ground for methods in pedagogy. What mattered most was acquiring a substantial amount of theoretical and factual wisdom in one's chosen area of study. The manner in which an instructor presented course material was hardly as important as the content of what would be conveyed in the classroom. For those of us without any formal training in pedagogy our methods of instruction and the contents of our course material often seemed to mirror the teaching customs of those professors we thought to be effective during our own post-secondary educational years. According to Maryann Cusimano, one advocate of active learning, the style of pedagogy we most often emulate endeavors us to be "effective, compelling, and entertaining lecturers, or good communicators of the vast stores of information we possess." For many of us, our teaching "mentors" were predominately men bearing well-worn file folders laden with a semester's worth of content material. Rarely did the contents of those file folders include issues pertaining to gender and their relationship to the various topical courses of the field. Even far more infrequent was the professor who would make a conscious attempt to involve the women of the class in a meaningful way.

The drawback to this method of transmitting information amounts to a teaching style that is extensively lecture-driven with the instructor occupying center stage. Students are involved in the learning process only to the extent that they transfer information from pen to notebooks. While we are often effective at delivering content, we rarely consider "alternative pedagogical methods" that could enhance our productiveness in the classroom and enable students to learn effectively by actively involving them in the learning process.[5] Before I became conscious of the importance of gender and its relationship to learning differences, I first began to explore a variety of teaching methods that I believed would allow the diversity of all students to become active participants in the learning process. Despite my well-intended aim, my initial attempts to initiate active learning could be best described as provincial. As an addition to my content filled lectures, students in my IR classes "actively" participated during the last few weeks of the term by orally presenting to the class their semester-long research projects. In retrospect, their class presentations turned out to be an imitation of the content delivery teaching method that I had exposed them to all semester long. Essentially, students "lectured" their fellow peers in 15 minute segments. Their classmates were rarely involved in the process unless someone either dared to ask a question or to put the speaker on notice that their voice was not being heard in the back of the room. Furthermore, I based my formula for evaluating their alleged "active" participation on the student's ability to intelligently present a specified quantity of information within a given amount of time.

In hindsight, this was not the active learning environment that I had hoped to attain. The women in these "active" classroom settings were less than comfortable with this type of course format whereas their male counterparts, regardless of race or ethnicity, seemed to relish their 15 minutes of fame. Not surprisingly, the women students neither researched gender specific topics in world politics, nor did they apply a gender-based methodology to their research. I have no doubt that this peculiarity was partly related to the absence of gender as an essential component of my course material at that time. On a few occasions, women students in a class on foreign policy would select a topic that involved women leaders such as Margaret Thatcher or Golda Meir. However, their analyses of specific foreign policy decisions formulated by these particular leaders remained cloaked in male constructs of permissible and appropriate international political behavior. After several dismal attempts at implementing what I thought was an active learning environment, I realized that not only was I failing on this front but my intent to advance critical thinking as a teaching goal was also receiving low marks.

Critical Thinking and Case Studies

Most university professors would acknowledge that one of their chief objectives is to foster critical thinking on the part of students. However, if critical thinking is broadly defined as the formation of one's own independent interpretation of a given issue after weighing the logic, accuracy, and persuasiveness of competing points of view, then the development of critical thinking in a lecture-driven classroom is a solitary exercise. Unless an instructor calls upon students directly or sets aside class time for oral presentations, students typically get to demonstrate their self-acquired level of critical thinking in the research paper. While it is important to be able to effectively communicate ideas in written form, reliance on written work as an exclusive measurement of critical thinking has several drawbacks. In the first instance, individual oral presentations and research papers do not constitute an active learning environment. Secondly, the promotion of critical thinking mainly through individual research and solitary writing assignments does not actively include the women present in the classroom. Thirdly, even though some students may choose to research a topic on women in world affairs, this information is not disseminated to the remainder of the class unless the course material is filtered through a gender-sensitive lens. As a result, women and the saliency of gender continue to remain hidden from world affairs and the women in the classroom continue to be accommodated rather than included.

Despite these present-day observations, I still was far from substantively, methodologically, and pedagogically transforming my IR curriculum. The next step in my progression began with the goal of creating an active learning environment. It was at this time that I discovered the Pew Case Studies in International Affairs as an instructional tool for active learning in international relations education. As a pedagogic approach, the premise of the case study method is that students learn more by actively participating rather than passively taking notes. Cases in international affairs essentially present the students with a key international event usually in a descriptive, or narrative form. The narrations do not attempt to analyze a specific event nor do they advocate a particular solution or outcome to a global problem. Instead, it is left up to the students themselves to critically analyze the events, propose workable solutions and evaluate the results. The role of the instructor is to facilitate class discussion of the case typically by introducing thought provoking questions.[6]

The Pew Case studies are divided into two broad categories: "action-forcing" and "retrospective" cases. In the former, students are often asked to assume the actual role of a policy practitioner who is confronted with a compelling international problem. Not unlike actual decision makers, these types of cases situate students in classical decision making situations that require them to sift through incomplete information, formulate a list of possible options, assess the probable consequences of each option, and select the best outcome. Examples of action-forcing cases among the Institute's collection include "The Suez Crisis of 1956," the "1982 Mexican Debt Negotiations", and "The Cuban Missile Crisis". In contrast, retrospective cases provide the students with the actual decision taken by policy makers as well as the consequences of those decisions. The role of the students is to probe why an individual decision maker chose a particular option and to speculate about the probable outcomes had another policy option been chosen. Examples of retrospective cases include "The Fall of Marcos: A Problem in U.S. Foreign Policymaking" and "Should the Reagan Administration Have Signed the U.N. Convention on the Law of the Sea?"[7]

Depending on one's pedagogic goals, use of the case study method has its advantages and disadvantages. In both reading the literature and applying this method of instruction in international affairs, I can recite numerous endorsements for this pedagogic approach. In addition to promoting critical thinking, students get to exercise such skills as public speaking, particularly during the actual case presentation and discussion. Public discussion of the cases forces the students to develop logical arguments and persuade others of their points of view. Moreover, case discussions also advance group dynamic skills that sharpen the student's ability to interpret group signals, particularly during the case presentation. If we as instructors could expand our classroom objectives to include such goals as public speaking and group dynamic skills alongside critical thinking, I believe that our students would be better prepared for life beyond the classroom walls. Moreover, if we promote these three goals alongside our expanded course content material, our students would have a more appropriate and applicable foundation in international affairs.

Because policy is not formulated in a vacuum, the cases provide students with a "hands-on" understanding of international politics that would otherwise remain abstract in a traditional lecture format. However, advocates of the case study method do not recommend that cases replace conventional lectures; instead, they are intended to supplement and complement lecture. The number of cases an instructor employs in any one semester is a matter of individual preference. Generally, instructors often choose between three and six cases. Furthermore, it is also up to the instructor how much in-class time, if any, will be given to students to adequately prepare for the case discussion. One advantage to in-class preparation is that it increases the amount of time an instructor can devote to an active learning environment and developing group dynamic skills. Proponents of the case study method, however, vary with regard to how much emphasis they place on students working together in groups both during the preparatory phase of the case and during the actual presentation of the case itself. Even though most of the case studies teaching notes provide an instructor with study questions to intellectually stimulate students before the actual case discussion, the emphasis of the case study method is not on group work.[8] In addition to the above mentioned advantages, one of the more prominent acclaims was that the case teaching method "places the student at the center of the educational process" and gives them the responsibility for their own learning.

The benefits of the case study method promote noble pedagogic goals. Speaking from the voice of experience as one who has used the case study method, I appreciate their value for promoting critical thinking, public speaking, and even group dynamics. However, in the process of transforming my IR curriculum to include women both in the course material and in the classroom, I began to question who benefits from the content of the case material as well as which student the case studies method actually place at the center of the educational process. I soon came to the conclusion that unless there is a corresponding shift in classroom dynamics, this method of instruction does not necessarily insure that women will be included in the process of benefiting from these exercises.

With respect to content, after a careful survey of the collection of available cases from the Institute for the Study of Diplomacy, I began to detect an inherent male bias. With the exception of one recently acquired case examining the global effects of overpopulation, the overwhelming majority of cases are exclusively male oriented. The bulk of the cases primarily deal with socially constructed topics of masculine political behavior that revolve either around military or economic conflicts and other national security issues reminiscent of a realist perspective of international affairs. Clearly, I was not advancing my goal of promoting gender as a substantive and methodologically important component of IR nor was I actively including the women in the classroom if my choice of cases about crisis decision making remained limited to topics such as the Cuban Missile Crisis. I believe that to ask women students to assume the role of a male decision maker neither advances the substance of gender in the field nor does it methodologically allow women students to be included in the learning process on the basis of their gender. However, what was probably more disturbing was that I became aware of a peculiar reticence on the part of women students to verbally participate in the case discussions. Without tossing aside the notion that this phenomenon was exclusively a result of gender-based learning differences, I wanted to believe that women students were reluctant to verbally participate because the content of the case material blatantly excluded women. In my view the omission of women as political participants and the absence of gender related topics from the library of case studies only serves to reinforce masculine constructs of international politics. Consequently, students of IR continue to receive and perhaps, regrettably receive, an incomplete picture of world politics while women and gender remain hidden. Regarding the classroom dynamics of case study discussion, there exists a tendency to perpetuate a competitive learning environment that excludes the active and equitable participation of women. Specifically, many of the action-forcing cases are inclined to create an adversarial classroom environment that disadvantages women and other minorities.[9] To overcome these drawbacks and using the existing cases as a guide, I began to devise new cases that would be appropriate for the gender aware IR curriculum that was beginning to take shape. I also began to examine the structure and composition of the groups working on improvised case study material. In addition to the change of case study content, I was now committed to developing a classroom environment that promoted cultural diversity and allowed for the full and equitable participation of all students.

Multiculturalism and Collaborative Learning

It was at this time that I came across two themes, one a pedagogic approach and the other a framework for analyzing intergroup relations that would comprise the last stage of transforming my IR curriculum. The idea that students claim responsibility for their own learning is one of the premises behind the collaborative learning approach. The major assumption of this pedagogic technique is that students work together in small groups toward a common goal. Although the foundation of collaborative learning differs from the case study method of instruction, these pedagogic techniques share certain similarities. Among these similarities are the promotion of critical thinking and the fact that the students are at center stage of the learning process rather than the instructor. However, while the case study method does not accentuate group learning, collaborative learning is built upon this premise.

The literature on collaborative learning recited numerous benefits that students acquire from actually working with their peers. In addition to critical thinking, students working in teams actually retain more information than students engrossed in solitary assignments.[10] Research on this type of learning environment provided a checklist of added collaborative learning benefits that includes higher achievement, increased self-esteem, decreased absenteeism, increased rates of retention, and more positive attitudes toward the subject matter.[11] Additionally, because collaborative learning gives students some degree of responsibility for their own learning while engaged in small group discussions, they are more likely to analyze and evaluate the variety of viewpoints and concepts they encounter. Consequently, the students may often be required to invoke as well as sharpen their problem-solving and conflict negotiation skills particularly in the IR classroom.

Organizing students into small groups to analyze case studies in international affairs would prove to be the easy part. The difficult part was developing gender aware cases and structuring groups to permit women to overcome their apparent reluctance to actively engage in the case study discussions. However, it is erroneous to assume that just by organizing students into small, culturally diverse groups that women and other minorities will readily and equitably participate. It is up to the instructor to ensure that "roles within groups do not play out stereotypes based on gender and race". In addition to assigning students to specific groups to safeguard against such tendencies, an instructor can draw on a number of evaluative standards to measure participation within groups.[12]

In formulating more gender-oriented case studies for analysis by small groups of culturally diverse students, I relied on the tenets of multiculturalism to help transform both my IR curriculum and the dynamics of classroom groups. Multiculturalism and its belief in the importance of recognizing, understanding, and respecting cultural differences based on gender, race, religion, age, and socio-economic status provided me with an appropriate theoretical foundation by which I could begin to actively include women and other minorities present in the classroom. Moreover, multiculturalism also proved to be the theoretical vehicle that finally led to a completely transformed IR curriculum along a more global and gender-based dimension.

According to Gordan and Newfield, multiculturalism has established itself as a framework for analyzing intergroup relations in the United States. Moreover, multiculturalism's influence has been discernible in a number of cultural, social, academic, and political circles where its meaningfulness and effects continue to spawn considerable debate. At the conceptual level, the controversy over multiculturalism tends to revolve around the lack of a congruent definition even among the diverse supporters of its use. What many of the supporting definitions appear to embrace is an overwhelming objection to the dominance of Western European values that have held command over the social, political, and economic fabric of American life at the expense of racial minorities and women.[13]

Alongside this rejectionist element there also seems to reside an inherent collective consciousness among many advocates of multiculturalism that acknowledges the importance of recognizing, understanding, and respecting cultural diversity in a democratic society. However, collective consciousness aside, debate over multiculturalism is also extant over the means by which we are to achieve cultural awareness. The realm of academia has not been immune from the discourse over the means and methods of promoting cultural diversity, especially in the classroom.[14]

Despite the variety of pedagogical approaches espoused for attaining cultural diversity in the classroom, I believe that multiculturalism should not be confined to "teaching" cultural diversity that is specific to issues of race and gender solely within the geographic region of the United States. Instead, student awareness, respect, and understanding of cultural diversity should endeavor to encompass a more global scope, particularly in an IR classroom environment. The idea of promoting a multi-cultural curriculum focus within IR forces us not only to address the absence of gender, but it allows us to redefine and expand the political playing grounds of the international system to include culture as a political variable. Cultural politics not only includes gender both substantively and methodologically, but also religion, ethnicity, nationalism, and so on. Culture in any society becomes the vehicle for the transmission of our social, sexual, and political identity and it is often at the root of most conflict in the world today. Culture, therefore, is not just a product of a society that defines who we are, but an ongoing process that sustains or alters the lenses through which we view the world.[15]

A multi-cultural approach to IR would provide a more complete view of international politics because it would establish a linkage between societal factors that includes gender and world affairs. Moreover, this type of approach allows us to develop cases for use in a collaborative learning environment that are applicable in the contemporary world and fit the theoretical concepts of the field. The problems that we confront today are more global in scope and have more far-reaching implications than many of the masculine constructed retrospective or action-forcing cases that tend to support the realist version of international affairs. Among the many contemporary issues that I have devised "case studies" for use in a collaborative IR classroom environment include global environmental issues, international migration, democratization, ethnic cleansing, as well as political and economic development. Students not only view these issues through a substantive and methodological gender filter, but also from competing socio-economic variables present in any given political situation.

I have noticed a number of immediate benefits that have resulted from extending the tenets of multiculturalism to a collaborative learning IR classroom environment. The most noticeable improvement has been the active participation of women students in the many discussion portions of the class. Moreover, it appears that many women students have also cast off their previous reticence even when discussions revolve around more traditional themes of the field such as war, the use of force, and crisis decision making. Without preaching feminism, women and other minorities no longer seem to sit silently and accept international relations as a world defined by European males in a collaborative learning environment that emphasizes global diversity.

Conclusion

Its a rare occasion when I'm asked a question by a student or colleague that expresses an interest in how I will teach a particular course as opposed to what topics a course will cover in a given semester. The lack of attention given to the methods of how we instruct over the substance of what we teach in the IR classroom does not trouble me as much as it used to in the past. Throughout my own evolution at establishing a multicultural, collaborative learning environment in the field of IR, I have come to realize that the substance of the course material is equally as important as the method of delivery. In the contemporary world of international politics the substance of gender is too important to be overlooked.

As noted in the introduction, gender matters. More importantly, it matters whether or not the substance of gender in world affairs focuses attention on women as foreign policy elites or women in a rural village who form a local cooperative to ensure themselves and their families a relative decent standard of living. Gender also matters in the IR classroom particularly when women are not consciously included or when there is a hesitancy on the part of women students to participate fully in the class.

Even though I believe that we have still a lot of territory to conquer before a woman-centered university will become a concrete reality, I nonetheless believe that the energy needed to spark a critical mass has taken root. As we continue our efforts at transformation in the classroom, I remain positive that our efforts will help to inspire others, including our students who may someday demand more from our educational system than the Euro-centric definition of world affairs.

Notes

1. Enloe, Cynthia. 1989. *Bananas, Beaches, and Bases: Making Feminist Sense of International Poltics.* Berkeley: University of California Press.

2. Sarkees, Meredith Reid and Nancy McGlen. 1995. "Backlash Toward Studying the Status of Women in Political Science and International Studies." Paper presented at the annual meeting of the International Studies Association, Chicago, IL.

3. Peterson, V. Spike and Anne Sisson Runyon. 1993. *Global Gender Issues.* Boulder: CO: Westview Press.

4. Bretherton, Charlotte. 1996. "Global Environmental Politics: The Gendered Agenda." Paper presented at the annual meeting of the International Studies Association, San Diego, CA.

5. Cusimano, Marayann K. 1995. "Why Do You Do What You Do the Way You Do It? Examining Teaching Goals and Teaching Methods." http://www.csf.colorado.edu/CaseNet/

6. Grecich, David G. and Peter E. Paraschos. 1996. "Reinventing International Affairs Education? Active Learning, the Case Method, and Case Studies." Pew Case Studies in International Affairs and the Institute for the Study of Diplomacy, Georgetown University, Washington, DC.

7. Greich, David G. and Peter E. Paraschos. 1996.

8. Franko, Patrice and Mark Boyer. 1995. "The ABC's of Case Teaching: a Manual in Progress." Paper presented at the annual meeting of the International Studies Association, Chicago, IL.

9. Sandler, Bernice Resnick, Lisa Silverbery, and Roberta Hall. 1996. *The Chilly Classroom Climate: A Guide to Improve the Education of Women.* Washington, DC: National Association for Women in Education.

10. Gokhale, Anuradha A. 1995. "Collaborative Learning Enhances Critical Thinking." *Journal of Technology Education*, 7: 4.

11. Sandler, et. al., 1996.

12. Sandler, et. al., 1996.

13. Gordon, Avery F. and Christopher Newfield, eds. 1996. *Mapping Multiculturalism.* Michigan: University of Minnesota Press.

14. Gordon, Avery F. and Christopher Newfield, eds., 1996.

15. Jordan, Glenn and Chris Weedon. 1995. *Cultural Politics: Class, Gender, Race, and the Postmodern World.* Cambridge, MA: Basil Blackwell.

Chapter 6

Teaching Cultural Diversity: Changing Classroom Dynamics

Helen Johnson

> If we examine critically the traditional role of the university in
> the pursuit of truth and the sharing of knowledge and information,
> it is painfully clear that biases that uphold and maintain white
> supremacy, imperialism, sexism and racism have distorted
> education so that it is no longer about the practice of freedom.
> The call for a recognition of cultural diversity, a rethinking of
> ways of knowing, a deconstruction of old epistemologies, and the
> concomitant demand that there be a transformation in our
> classrooms, in how we teach and what we teach, has been a
> necessary revolution. (hooks 1994: 29 - 30).

Breaking Down Barriers

Why situate women in Anthropology? How do the changing
demographics of a university's student body change teaching and
learning practices? Why teach courses that examine cultural diversity
and differing concepts of gender? What are students' attitudes to
theories that deconstruct domination, racism, sexism, class
exploitation, and colonial practices? How can our learning
experiences as teachers and students together deconstruct prevailing
stereotypes of feminists and promote potentialities for social change?
As an anthropologist who has researched gender issues in Europe and
the Pacific, as well as retaining a lively interest in the theoretical
transformation and elaboration of a variety of feminist theories, I am

fortunate to be able to teach a variety of courses both within the discipline of Anthropology and from the cross-disciplinary perspectives of Women's Studies. In this article I reflect on a course: Race and Sexual Politics: Questioning Concepts and Categories.[1] I use the course in order to account for, and ground, the kinds of pedagogic issues that I am discussing here. The course engages a range of theoretical and ethnographic materials chosen to empower students to understand the differing ways in which power and domination can shape both our predominant conceptualizations of women and men, and the material relations within which women and men experience their lives, particularly in non-western cultures. The course guides students through an intellectual and cognitive encounter with the unfamiliar, and a questioning of the 'exotic', the 'primitive', and the 'alien'. Video and textual materials illustrate to students the differences and diversities which are encompassed by 'other' cultures, as well as the gendered, racialized, sexualized, and ageist concepts that work to construct peoples lived realities. The course proposes and examines sometimes tragic yet often astonishing visions of the forceful processes of transnationalism and globalization and how they are refashioning the cultural and social elements and interactions of Australia as a diverse and changing society, and those of our Asian and Pacific Rim neighbors. The course works towards a deeper appreciation of what may be gained by understanding other ways of life.

As part of my pedagogic philosophy, I encourage students to develop an understanding of the complex theoretical and political problems that are generated by studying and writing about feminist and gender issues within and across different cultures. Philomena Essed proposes that it is important to *"make implicit boundaries explicit* before they can be challenged" (Essed 1994: 232, her emphasis). Ideas within feminist poststructuralism have, for a number of reasons, principally shaped the analytical perspectives that have been adopted for the course discussed here. Not only do ideas encompassed by feminist poststructuralism enable explorations of how women actively position themselves in discourses that can oppress and subordinate them, they contribute to analyses of the workings of patriarchal structures, organizations, credos and values.

However, the power of concepts generated within feminist poststructuralism is significantly enhanced by anthropological perspectives that bring contemporary feminist theory into dialogue with current issues in cultural anthropology. Although in Women's Studies women are placed at courses' discursive centers, most students are not unsettled by this focus, as other courses taken as part of their undergraduate studies have usually destabilized their socialization into the restrictions of patriarchal scholarship. In subtle contrast however, within the conceptual frame of Anthropology, many courses work to sustain an appreciation of cultural difference amongst women and men, not as unreasoning cultural relativism, but as a recognition and elaboration of differently situated and gendered perspectives, understandings, and discernments. By conflating the two approaches in my pedagogic practice it is possible, as Essed contends, to break through disciplinary and epistemological boundaries to "encourage students to foster a global perspective on race and on issues of ethnicity and gender" to develop constructive dialogues (Essed 1994: 233).

The Challenge of Teaching and Learning about Cultural Diversity through Theory and Issues

How do the changing demographics of a university's student body change teaching and learning practices? Australia's location as a neighbor to Southeast Asian and Pacific nations, and its history as a colonized outpost of British Imperialism, means that its universities are uniquely placed to generate a productive pedagogy and to explore the challenges and tensions generated through local, national, regional, and international developments. Indeed, an exploration of 'women's worlds' has been timely. It timeliness is not just the result of the emergence of gay and lesbian studies, Koorie (Aboriginal) Studies, and interest in gender issues that emerged during the past decade. It is also because the lingering effect of bigoted stereotypes is presently causing bitter dispute amongst Australians as a new political party titled One Nation gains ground for racist assumptions in a climate of fear and economic adversity. In addition, recent Australian governments during the 1980s have promoted a political and commercial desire to expand into the burgeoning economies of Southeast Asia. As Dever (1996) contends, throughout that decade prevailing understandings of what it meant to be 'Australian' and what it meant (from Australia's point of view) to be 'Asian' were destabilized by increased migration from the diverse countries of Southeast Asia, an official government policy of multiculturalism, and powerful Aboriginal challenges to ascendant and authoritarian narratives of white history.

Coterminously, the swift economic development of the Newly Industrializing Countries of the Asian region "transformed the comfortable, imperialist accounts of 'Asian' dependence and passivity into persuasive new narratives of power and capital. These, narratives threatened to shatter forever Australia's lingering fantasies of economic prosperity, regional dominance, and racial superiority" (Dever 1996: 2). A desire by Australia's government to enmesh itself with Asia to unashamedly ride upon the coat-tails of its economic growth, has in the 1990s transmogrified into a potentially neo-colonialist strategy of national aggrandizement. As such, the recently elected Howard government is moving to place new restrictions on immigration to ensure that Australia remains 'Australian' whilst resisting the notion that Asia could/should be a part of Australia (Dever 1996).

While Australia's desire to merge economically with Asia may be harnessed due to the recent collapse of the economies of Thailand and Malaysia, Australia's tendency to conceptualize and conflate the diverse geopolitical and sociocultural components of 'Asia' into an undifferentiated totality works, nevertheless, to mask the complex realities of women's lived experiences in this region. It is these sociopolitical factors which substantiate a self-reflexive examination of the power of 'Western' discourses in relation to the political and philosophical interests of people in our neighboring countries. Students become exposed to international and cross-cultural materials through their own lived experience as 'Asian students', or their interactions with students from non-Australian backgrounds.

Why do I teach courses that examine cross-cultural diversity and differing concepts of gender? For me, it is important to share the excitement of insights and understandings from 'other' cultures and our own, to construct strategies to combat Australia's potential xenophobia, and to assist in the generation of critical reflections on social and cultural relations of power. From my students I am assuming a prior knowledge of some anthropological and comparative social theory, but few skills in critical reading, analysis, and conceptual thinking. Consequently, I use this basis for the creation and analysis of theory that is anchored in a sociocultural appreciation of women's diverse material realities and subjective lived experiences. As hooks contends, "what we are witnessing today in our everyday life is not an eagerness on the part of neighbors and strangers to develop a world perspective but a return to narrow nationalism, isolationisms, and xenophobia" (hooks 1994: 29). In acknowledging these sociopolitical biases I work to minimize the difficulties that many students encounter when challenged to think about 'the collective cultural consumption' of ideas. Kathleen Dunn has astutely analyzed the affective barriers raised by students who may

> withdraw from a learning situation when they encounter material that challenges their existing values system. Since material in women's studies courses can challenge the value systems of young women who have been raised in traditional families, this is also a barrier to which teachers need to be sensitive. In order to prevent students from ignoring or dismissing new material that challenges their religious, cultural, or personal belief systems, a teacher can structure discussion and small group opportunities with specific assignments to give all students a change to explore and formulate in a critical way their position on the given issue. (Dunn 1993:40)

Students often hold the view that not only are their own thoughts and lived experiences not important enough to be incorporated into theoretical endeavor, but that theory is 'beyond' them. Some tell me that they can negotiate 'practical' problems, but lack the confidence to formulate or question concepts. To reinforce my contention that theory is principally about the ways in which people interpret reality, and that, as scholars we must understand the importance of interpretation as well as the need for speculation, the course promotes an understanding of the creation and production of knowledge that uncovers the power relations inherent in 'knowing' others. This is socially appropriate as the students' cultural diversity and heritage reflect the rapidly changing social and cultural demographics of the university's student body as a whole. I have observed the composition of students to be approximately 60 percent 'Australian' - comprising students of Italian, Greek, Vietnamese, Malaysian, Indonesian, Singaporean, and Eastern European heritage - and 40 percent fee-paying students from South-East Asian countries who are studying in Australia in order to return to their home countries with the prestige of a degree from an overseas institution. A positive outcome from the increasing diversity of the university's student body has been that students who carry with them different assumptions about the teaching and learning process challenge conventional notions about teaching practice and prompt an exploration of new and inclusive ways of knowing. Furthermore, discussion of issues such as 'race', 'gender' and 'power' need to be well-grounded in phenomena to which a diverse student body can relate. Seminars addressing the growth of sex tourism as an industry in countries such as Thailand and the Philippines, as well as the use of 'entertainers' and 'escorts' in Japan, Taiwan, and Australia create fundamental linkages with actual experiences that students can observe in their home communities and/or whilst travelling. Their own experiences of cross-border travel and cross-cultural romantic liaisons generate an interest in debates about AIDS, and power relations inherent in employer/maid relationships find resonance in discussions of the lives and conditions of Filipina maids. Theoretical insights into the power/knowledge nexus are generated by Australian debates about Aboriginal self-determination, Native Title, indigenous land rights, and discussions of the 'stolen children' taken from their Aboriginal mothers in the 1950s to be placed in government institutions of 'care'. Such grounded social phenomena link with my primary concern, which is to ensure that students perceive that power is enacted through gender differences. I work to enable the students to understand that many social forces can intersect in women and men's lives in culturally specific, philosophically contentious, yet often oppressive ways.

Classroom analyses of video material such as *Babakueria* (1994), *The Good Woman of Bangkok* (1993), and *Rap, Race, and Equality* (1996) show explicitly how women's life choices, bodily practices, and very survival are shaped by specific sociocultural practices such as the construction of racialized and sexualized categories of 'the primitive', the globalization and capitalism and the physical expression of male power, and racialized and gendered state intervention in family and reproductive policies. A Bangladeshi video titled *Eclipse* (1995) portrays the ways in which Islamic fundamentalist men destroy the small economic projects set up by poor women in conjunction with non-government organizations. The uprooting of mulberry trees planted on common ground along the roadways to provide silkworms, is a concrete action designed to ensure that women remain in the home. Yet the women are not passively silent. They vigorously protest their loss of income, querying who will buy food for their children. The film enables students to recognize the ways that unauthorized 'fundamentalist' male power over women can tarnish women's lived experiences, their very potential to survive, as well as many social relations. After viewing these videos several students have expressed their fresh awareness that 'there is so much work to do'. For me, their awareness is heartening. For I believe a major goal for feminist educators must surely be to maintain the challenge to racist and sexist practices by disseminating the need to examine and analyze policy decisions and outcomes, both within our home countries, and those of our neighbors. The topics are presented in ways that are designed to deconstruct the unspoken assumptions that men and women respond in the same way to sexualized, gendered, racialized, and nationalized conflict, and to issues of self-interest. The students exchange views, which encounter, acknowledge and occasionally release racial tensions and cultural differences. The materials I provide acknowledge the important differences of skin color, nationality, and class among women, both as a reality and a symbol of cultural difference. For example, material describing lynchings and the sexual use of black women's bodies during slavery, the phenomena of femicide and dowry-deaths in India, and the rigidly enforced dress-codes of some Islamic cultures, often produces forceful reactions from young women. They are repulsed by the psychological and physical brutality imposed upon young women's sexuality, as well as interpretations of religious teachings which, for them, are blatantly shaped by male self-interest. However, the material is helpful for showing how women's differing bodily practices, as well as women's differing histories can be linked in a powerful exposé of the difficulties of positing a global sisterhood. Deconstructing ideas about a global sisterhood has meant the students need to consider who has the power to speak for whom, and whether some women have sufficient social presence to enable their counter-hegemonic narratives to be heard. Course materials also consider the ways in which women can recognize difference without necessarily constructing division, and thereby work together in, what Chandra Mohanty calls, 'an international coalition' of like-minded scholars and activists, to achieve social change and social justice. In these ways I cautiously and optimistically operate with the notion of women working together, recognizing difference as diversity rather than division, and taking seriously the politics of knowledge production. The students come to understand that women forge common ground contingently rather than through a putative solidarity.

The political relationship between 'First World' scholars' desire to understand 'Third World' peoples is addressed, using the works of critics such as Donna Haraway (1989, 1991) bell hooks (1981, 1984), Chandra Mohanty (1991), Jan Jindy Pettman (1992, 1996), and Marianna Torgovnick (1991, 1997). Their work provokes insights into the ways that patterns of power can play out upon women's bodies in different ways. Contentious and confronting issues such as the social phenomena of prostitution, sex tourism, and the sexual harassment of women of color are examined in ways which explore their complex nature and which allow students to recognize the dilemmas inherent in discerning the values, beliefs and practices of other peoples. Ethnographic representations are used to examine the problems of 'seeing' AIDS and the ways that stereotypic notions of 'race', 'gender', and 'sexuality' link with the difficulties of visually, textually, and politically representing women and men of color. Such issues are used to treat the psychosocial and sexual dynamics of the feminist classroom as a site where the political struggle over meaning can be part of a project to self-consciously examine, question, and develop critical understandings of gender relations. Such an approach works towards conscious transformations in the demeanor, subjectivity, and practice of the student.

Textual materials support the videos and works such as Mary Bateson's (1994) *Peripheral Visions: learning along the way,* as well as Mary Hawkesworth's (1989) "Knowers, Knowing, Known: Feminist theory and claims of truth" that give additional examples of the ways in which imaginative reasoning can be stifled by the need and desire to be 'correct' within particular sociocultural frames.

Students' Attitudes Toward Theory

Whilst hooks quite justifiably brings our attention to the disruptive potential of 'exciting' higher education (hooks 1994: 7) most students in my teaching experience have appeared to be as positively and radically excited by the unfolding of new concepts as I am. Nonetheless, some have articulated their sense of being overwhelmed by the magnitude and complexity of the sociocultural processes that they must analyze and the quantity and content of the theories presented. Certainly, some have told me that they find some postcolonial material to be 'too difficult'. However, others are stimulated by the application of feminist and anthropological analyses to women's formative lived experience which has, in turn, generated their need to engage in an active politics.

The challenges of theory may appear complicated for young people, and for women in particular. Fortunately, feminist poststructuralism has enlarged the space of discourse and, in turn, has opened up pedagogical discourse in humane and liberating ways. Hence, the theoretical implications of the politicization of cultural practices such as female genital mutilation are discussed in ways that enhance students' understanding of the 'practical' concerns of the procedure. They express much heartache and concern as they try to adapt often strongly felt antipathy, as women, to the terms of their earlier training in cultural relativism, and then pivot once more to new intellectual understandings of women's concerns in different cultures.

As poststructural feminism also emphasizes the creation of new ways of seeing and knowing, feminist poststructuralist theories can be used to clarify political problems. It has the capacity to provide detailed analyses of the workings of patriarchy in its psychosocial manifestations: structural, institutional, organizational, ideological, and subjective. It enables social relations to be viewed in terms of plurality and diversity rather than unity and imposed consensus, to enable an articulation of alternative, more effective ways of thinking about or acting on issues of gender. It recognizes that 'agency' is of equal importance to structures, organizations and processes in the production of social practices, and that people are not passively socialized into their individual worlds, but actively compose the discursive constructions through which they are shaped.

Resistance to Populist Stereotypes of Feminists

How is my teaching approach different to that which hooks categorizes as "the traditional role of the university in pursuit of truth and the sharing of knowledge and information"? (hooks 1994: 29). I situate myself as a white feminist anthropologist in relation to course materials in an attempt to destabilize established perceptions of a teacher disseminating information. I talk of my own involvement in politics and community work as well as academically anchored philosophical theorizing, in order to enable students to understand that the two are not a binary opposition which creates mutual exclusion, but an interactive and progressive process. I tell my students of the women's groups which are moving beyond one-time interventions that rarely work and which tend to leave the women's organization open to accusation of grand-standing by women in need of real aid. I highlight the women who truly want to make a difference, in their being willing to develop long-term relationships with local community, as well as international, groups and organizations that are already in touch with the cultural needs of those people whom they are meant to serve. Yet I also underscore the need to think creatively about our lived realities, rather than try to ascertain the 'right' way to go about things, particularly in political action.

I construct learning assessments that encourage a deep learning approach that is critical, progressive and life-long. And, while I have not conducted fieldwork in 'Asian' countries, I interweave the theoretical framework of melding philosophical considerations and anthropological can-do approaches with my pedagogical ideals of not territorializing, nor politically gerrymandering, courses, issues, and research topics. Wilson and Russell have queried the efficacy of criticizing women who teach courses and do research not derived from their own experiences, a position which found resonance with my pedagogic ideals. Consequently, I not only attempt to be supportive to my institutional colleagues, but to be sensitive to students who are engaging profoundly with cross-cultural material which frequently 'tilts' their view of reality and undermines their received ideas. One of my students - a Malaysian woman in her early '30s - told me that she and her younger Southeast Asian colleagues admired my approach. Not only did they not expect support for their home cultures from a white woman, they told me that they had never met a white woman who critiqued her own culture and the social inequities which supported white people's status in their home communities. Their perceptions of my status as a white female university lecturer, and their experiences with strong hierarchies of power in their home communities where certain kinds of wealthy, educated, class-privileged women maintained established hierarchies of oppression, suggested to them that I should be reinforcing my position, rather than stimulating them to question it. I found their observation to be gratifying in two ways. First, it shows a potential way in which feminist teachers can work against populist promotions of feminist intolerance and representations of disapproving maternalist orthodoxies. Finding that many young women were intimidated by deprecating stereotypes of feminist women, I do not validate one particular type of self-presentation but prefer to stimulate discussion about popular culture representations of feminists and feminist academics. Such representations can work in powerful linkages to limit students' desire to engage with the constructive body of ideas and practices that feminism generates. Second, the woman's observation signaled to me the students' move away from a perception that they had no authority to speak, to a working through of a subjective perception of the injustice of their social location. Their observation substantiates the paradigm shift that is occurring in feminist pedagogy from teaching to learning. They are moving towards what Begnal elucidates as a connective and constructivist knowing in which they were learning to trust in their personal authority to know, "an authority based on the primacy of experience, of one's lived and felt perceptions" (Begnal 1991: 289).

Students are consequently confronting dominant models of feminism, and elite women's authority in their own culture. Their self-reflexive situation of their experience produces knowledge rather than belittles them as the passive recipients of knowledge transfer preferred by the 'authoritative' and 'authoritarian' patriarchal model. My non-authoritarian approach to mentoring students creates a different kind of learning environment for them. Not only is my model of teaching more negotiated than an authoritative model, their experience of institutional flexibility and interactions between equals can act to change their approach to their wider culture. Such a pedagogic philosophy works towards creating a safe environment in which students are enabled to explore long-held assumptions.

To mitigate the intolerance and ignorance of feminism which is prevalent in mainstream Australian media and to provide them with an understanding of the nexus between the academic and the popular, I encourage a critical analysis of popular culture stereotypes, prompting my students to become critical consumers of media representations. As Wilson and Russell contend, "[a]s long as the images of girls and women in children's books, on television, and in films and magazines focus on racial and gender stereotypes, the attitudes and perspectives of the past will be perpetuated" (Wilson and Russell 1996: 273). The material is provided to urge them to question why female characters are represented as 'more vain or less heroic' than their male counterparts, and why women of color in particular, are either missing or given lesser credit. Examinations of how knowledge is made entails the students understanding what it means to be a 'woman' at different moments in history, and in different cultures. Often young people, particularly women, perceive that they are not supposed to think analytically about society, or to question contemporary structures and organizations, or to consider how our lived realities could be different. In prompting students to take a more active conscious relationship to their world, I help them perceive how to negotiate and change the structures and policies that shape, and frequently control, their lives.

Potentialities for Social Change and Social Justice

The course promotes discussion in which students provide anecdotal evidence from their own experience in Southeast Asian cultures from the national and local perspective, and Australian women provide anecdotes and examples from their travels. Their articulations enable a powerful transformative pedagogy to anchor itself in a respect for multiculturalism whilst being critically aware of its pitfalls. As Freire (1970) and hooks (1994) have proposed, "we must build 'community' in order to create a climate of openness and intellectual rigour" (hooks 1994: 40). In this way not only do I as the educator, teach by telling stories, but the students also contribute, as Pagano asserts, to telling "stories about knowledge, about what it is to be a human knower, about how knowledge is made, claimed, and legitimated" (Pagano 1994: 252).

Pedagogically this practice enables me not only to learn different ways of knowing but also to displace myself as the primary and authoritative voice. Lensink has poignantly asserted that one must be prepared "to give up the authority of the teacher in the classroom, to admit the limits of [one's] knowledge freely to [one's] students, to enable students to learn from each other, and to learn to respect each other's knowledge and lived experience" (Lensink 1991: 279). The shift from my authoritative voice to one of student's finding their own is enhanced by floating sessions programmed towards the end of each semester which are designed to inspire students to gain confidence in the oral presentation of their work-in-progress.

The practice of telling stories articulates the theories that embrace our assumptions about reality and shows how theory can link with everyday life. Bunch has provocatively asserted that, "[t]heory helps to clarify how things work and what our choices are, and thus aids in determining where to put our energies and how to challenge the sources of our oppression most effectively" (Bunch 1987: 247). Like many of my female colleagues working in education, I am interested in the ways in which the educational process intersects with potentialities for social change. In particular, I am concerned with the connections between feminist politics and the role which education can play in the development of individuals and societies with a commitment to social justice. As Hughes has argued, "the development of critical consciousness which facilitates understanding of the operation of power structures" is central to the educational process (Hughes 1996: 103). For me, the process of developing a penetrating analysis of power moves beyond the limitations of the empowerment and development of critical capacities only in individuals, to feed into the broader potentialities of social action for change. It is, I believe, important for students to understand that the movement beyond individual awareness can transform the structures that maintain oppression (Hughes 1996:104). In revealing the hierarchies that constitute institutions and structures of the state and those that also shape many social organizations, I present ethnographic examples of women's resistance, particularly those of 'indigenous' peoples. Using Lila Abu-Lughod's (1990) article "*the romance of resistance: tracing transformations of power through Bedouin women*"; Maria Jaschok and Suzanne Miers' (1994) *Women and Chinese Patriarchy;* and material addressing Australian Aboriginal peoples' claim to land under Native Title legislation, I found that students encounter and more profoundly understand the complex interplay of global, regional, national, local, gendered, racialized, and classist power relations, as well as their potential for power imbalances.

In these ways students are given conceptual tools in terms of theories, explanations, and examples to further analyses of representational politics, to gain an understanding of the ways in which sociocultural practices shape bodily practices and subjectivities, and to develop students' theoretical and evaluative capacities to examine cultural differences and diverse phenomena. As importantly, the materials show women acting as social agents, negotiating relations of power, resisting domination, and celebrating their capabilities, representations which counter stereotypic images of women as solely 'victims' of oppressive structures and ideologies.

So where does the study of cultural diversity lead Australian and Southeast Asian students? It is my belief that explorations of peoples' lived experiences, their bodily practices, and their subjectivities across cultures can blur boundaries between 'self' and 'other' to foster empathy and, as Monk and her co-authors suggest, "a sense of common cause and commitment to supportive action" (Monk 1991: 246). The gift of conceptual tools that enables students to work towards their own very particular way of being and thinking, as well as the recognition of the dignity of others, can promote a future that has the plenitude of experience, emotion, and intellectual stimulation that enables them to engage in 'a life worth living'. For me, young women in particular, in recognizing and celebrating their diversity, may guide humanity into the next millennium.

Notes

1. This course was initially developed by my colleague Dr. Lucy Healey—I have been teaching it now for three years, revising and rethinking elements of it in the process.

Chapter 7

Using Inquiry and Children's Literature to Ask Hard Questions With Women in Education

Martha Foote and Carole Walker

> Our deepest fear is not that we are inadequate. Our deepest fear is that we are powerful beyond measure. It is our light and not our darkness that most frightens us. . . .There is nothing in life about shrinking so that others will not feel insecure around you. We are all meant to shine as children do. We are born to make visible the glory of God that is within us. It is not just in some of us, but in everyone. As we let our own light shine we unconsciously give others permission to do the same. As we are liberated from our fears our presence automatically liberates us.
> --Mary Ann Williamson

Gender equity, "a regard for the qualitative differences in the perspectives, needs and learning styles of the two sexes," is a factor in determining if individuals are able to become "powerful beyond measure".[1] Gender equity within a culture refers to all individuals having freedom from limits imposed by self or society that would prohibit both males and females from pursuing the fields of knowledge and skills suited for them. With the expansion of learning and achievement potentialities identified by Gardner's multiple intelligences theory, overall intelligence is coming to be seen as the ability to solve problems, ask new and valuable questions, and provide a product or service useful to humankind. Designing environments and instructional interventions to facilitate the development of powerful learners of both sexes must be a foremost goal for educators. Our task is one of allaying gender bias and enabling powerful individuals, capable of pushing their own personal boundaries and of tolerance for others to do the same, to flourish.

Where Are We Now?

For those of us training elementary teachers to teach, the findings from research related to gender equity in the school environment are generally disturbing. Evidence from four strands of gender-equity issues points up the subtle but pervasive sexism that exists in society and schools today. These strands are 1) teacher-student interactions; 2) gender differences in communication and play; 3) gender differences in academic achievement; and 4) equity in environment and curricular materials. "Gender inequity is the norm, and anything else is not normal"[2]

Teacher-Student Interactions

A consistent finding among studies in this area is that boys demand and receive more attention from their teachers. Boys not only receive more negative attention for their conduct, but have also been found to dominate teacher-student interaction time (Eccles and Blumenfeld 1985). In studying classroom interactions in over 100 fourth, fifth, and eighth grade classrooms over a four year period, Myra and David Sadker found that male students received more attention from teachers whether the teacher was male or female, Black or White. Other findings were that boys called out eight times more often than girls and that when teachers responded to boys they tended to accept their answers while responses to girls often included reminders to raise their hands. The Sadkers commented, "Boys are being trained to be assertive; girls are being trained to by passive--spectators relegated to the sidelines of classroom discussion"[3] They also found that boys received more specific, and therefore more instructive, feedback from teachers.

Gender Differences in Communication and Play

Maccoby examined the ways boys and girls talk with other children and concluded that girls' speech more often served the purpose of establishing or strengthening relationships; whereas, boys' speech was used mostly to assert their position or attract an audience (Stanford 1992). The establishment of gender role has been found to peak around age six when children tend to insist on almost over generalized, rigid expectations for masculine and feminine behavior (Maccoby 1974; Paley 1984). Still in question is whether this view can be attributed to an innate developmental milestone or to cognitive development within cultural socialization. Studies of children's play have revealed that self-imposed sex segregation occurs in early years (Lloyd and Smith 1985; Perry et al., 1993; Lewis 1991). However, Kyle Pruett, a researcher in the Yale Child Study Center, detected an anomaly in a longitudinal study of 16 families in which the fathers are the primary caregivers/nurturers and mothers work full-time outside the home.

> I saw boys really enjoy their nurturing skills....They knew what to do with a baby, they didn't see that as a girls' job, they saw it as a human job. I saw the girls have very active images of the outside world and what they mothers were doing in the workplace--things that become interesting to most girls when they're 8 or 10, but these girls were interested when they were 4 to 5 (Shapiro 1990: 65).

Investigating gender differences in older children's play, Lever (1978) concluded that 10 and 11-year old boys' games were longer, more complex, more competitive, and tended to be done in larger, more age-heterogeneous groups than did the games or play of girls providing them fewer opportunities to develop vital skills in higher level thinking, negotiation, teamwork, and leadership.

Gender Differences in Achievement

Most troubling of all, perhaps, is the reported gender differences between the achievement of boys and girls. According to the Sadkers and Long, "Girls are the only groups in our society that begins school ahead and ends school behind" (Sadklers 1989: 114-116). In their look at gender equity in the schools twenty-five years after the passage of title IX, they report that boys outperform girls on both the Scholastic Aptitude Test (SAT) and American College Testing Program Examination (ACT) with the largest difference in scores being in the mathematics section of the SAT. In contrast, math achievement in the elementary years has been found to slightly favor girls (Campbell 1986).

Equity in Environment and Curricular Materials

Elements of the physical surroundings, the teacher, and the curricular materials impact the realization of gender equity (Stanford 1992). The arrangement of seating within the room (i.e., randomly grouping boys and girls together imply expectations of interactions and equality; and avoiding hierarchical patterns which might imply higher gender status) can promote gender equity. Bulletin boards, posters, photographs and other types of classroom displays which depict equal representation of males and females in roles that "advertise the ideas and accomplishments of men and women in all areas of the curriculum" (Shapiro 1990: 98) are also associated with equitable physical surroundings.

Six areas of bias to look for when examining textbooks, literature or other curricular materials were identified in the Sex Equity Handbook for School (Sadker and Sadker 1982): invisibility, stereotyping, imbalance/selectivity, unreality, fragmentation/isolation, and linguistic bias. By being aware of these broad areas, teachers can involve students in recognizing discriminatory texts and can counter such texts with more gender-equitable ones. Wallace suggested that teachers rewrite blatantly stereotypical math problems that show women occupied with cooking and men in construction.

Basal texts used in elementary classrooms in the 1970s overwhelmingly showed boys as the central character (Blom et al., 1970; Graebner 1972; and Britton and Lumpin 1977). While the number of males in a central character role in six reading textbook series had dropped from 61 to 18 percent by the late 1980s, "the percentage of females...had remained virtually the same" (Hitchcock and Tompkins 1987: 289). Questions of sexism were avoided by creating neutral or neutered characters. Similarly, an early study of children's literature found females to be underrepresented and depicted in stereotypical roles (Fisher 1974). About ten years later,

Scott maintained that more gender equitable literature was available and found that "readers of materials in which males and females engage in nontraditional activities express fewer sex-typed responses about occupations, roles and traits than those who read about people in sex-typed roles" (Quay et al., 1993: 5).

The Intervention: Do Let Your Babies Grow Up to Be Cowgirls

An intervention designed to heighten awareness of gender inequities and promote powerful learning for all evolved over the past year and a half. This strategy allows individuals within groups to 1) generate hard questions related to gender, 2) use inquiry to test an hypothesis about the treatment of gender in children's literature, and 3) explore possibilities for further inquiry into gender issues. The content and methodology developed in a variety of settings that are part of the field-based teacher education program at our university. The authors teach two of the three junior-level, campus-based courses that precede two semesters of internship and residency. In addition, each leads a university liaison team, which designs and delivers the field-based seminars in two of the partner districts. Asking "hard" questions has increasingly become routine in our work with these teams and also with pre-service and in-service teachers in the variety of settings which the professional development school model affords.

These questions convey trust in others as learners, leaders, and researchers. The transition from the often passive role of students to the necessarily more active role of teacher is hastened by asking and answering questions of interest to the learner. The focus on questions models the possibility for using content other than the "mandated curriculum. . . loaded with someone else's voice asking all of the questions and demanding all of the answers" (Copenhaver 1993: 6). Use of the questioning process has the potential of leading (slowly) into the routine use of structured inquiry, not only in the public school classrooms, but also in staff development sessions in which the "teacher's questions about teaching and learning are the focus of the study" (Marshall and Hatcher 1996: 44). Asking "hard" questions through the inquiry process has even resulted in systematic work toward thoughtful solutions to the persisting problems which challenge school communities (Levin 1993).

The relative presence of gender bias in children's literature became the topic of choice for our work for several reasons. It fits rather naturally into one of the three core methods courses Reading 350: Reading and Language Arts in the Elementary School, which precedes the year in the field. Finding evidence to support an hypothesis about gender bias in the books of the 1990's is equally accessible--and of interest--to children and adults. The issue of gender bias is both suitably complex and readily transportable so that the inquiry process can continue in new settings of interest to the participants. With them goes the realization that whatever agreements we reach during the first inquiry are temporary, not final answers.

Twenty Questions More or Less: The Opening

The work begins with each of those assembled writing a question (Copenhaver 1993) in response to the prompt, "Regarding gender bias, my wonderful question is…" (see Figure 7.1). This is followed by space for telling why the question has importance to the writer. Then the questions and reasons are shared, sometimes with a partner or a small group, but often in turn with the total group. The opening is intended to be invitational, learner-centered, and active. In addition, it gives the facilitator a feel for the relative importance gender issues have for the group. Finally, the realization that questions of interest to the group drive the inquiry process is encouraged by this opening.

White Dynamite and Curly Kidd: The Book to Read Aloud.

This book by major children's author Bill Martin, Jr. whose home is within a few miles of our university, was chosen because it 1) is an excellent read-aloud book for two voices, and 2) the gender of the hero--a girl who aspires to be a rodeo rider--is not revealed until the last page when she pulls off her hat "letting her hair down." Experiencing children's literature almost always generates positive affect within a group of pre-service or in-service educators. While the gender bias questions and the issues surfacing as the questions were shared should have been unsettling, the following activity provides both a respite and a subtle reminder of the prevalence of gender stereotypes within our culture.

Figure 7.1
Gender Bias and Children's Literature

My name is
My two favorite children's books are • •
My wonderful question about gender bias and children's literature is
The reason it is important to me is

Gathering Data Related to a Gender Bias Hypothesis

The group is next randomly divided into groups based on even or odd numbered dates of birth to search for data (i.e., passages from respected children's books) to support--or reject--the following hypothesis: The hero of this book has become commonplace during this decade; there is no longer a need to be concerned about gender bias in children's literature. A number of children's book, chart paper, and markers are made available to the groups. A time limit of 30 minutes is imposed for the investigation. The random assignment usually ensures a diversity of opinions within the group so that the complexity of the issue and the challenge of gathering compelling evidence related to the hypothesis is heightened. Findings of each group are shared at the end of the first data collection effort during a "gallery walk." Those present walk around and view, as in a visit to an art gallery, the evidence of the other groups as depicted on their charts. Those participating in the "walk" may use self-adhesive notes to pose any hard questions to the makers of the charts. Following the walk, there is time for assessing and reflecting within the group. The final activity of this segment is to "vote with one's feet." Personal acceptance or rejection of the hypothesis about gender bias in children's literature is indicated by where within the room one chooses to stand.

Inquiry: The Process for the 21st Century

In the last few minutes, the pithy quotes in Figure 7.2 are shared. Conversations ensue about next steps regarding other venues and audiences for continuing investigation into gender bias in children's literature and using the inquiry process to answer hard questions.

Figure 7.2
Inquiry: The Process for School Improvement

> The Inquiry Process is a systematic method for solving the complex problems of a school community. It is a process that enables groups of people to work together to gain a more complete understanding of the challenges they face. Then, after a problem is understood fully, the process encourages collaboration, creativity and thoughtfulness as a school community constructs its own unique solutions.
>
> Henry M. Levin, Accelerated Schools Project
> Stanford University

Inquiry: The Process for Staff Development

> If teachers have opportunities for collaborative inquiry and learning, the vast wisdom of practice developed by excellent teachers will be shared across the profession.
>
> Linda Darling-Hammond, Educational Leadership 53 (6), p. 9
>
> Action research is structured inquiry in which the teacher's questions about teaching and learning are the focus of the study.
>
> Stephanie Pace Marshall and Connie Hatcher
> Educational Leadership 53 (6), p. 44

Our Experience With Our Intervention

This intervention has been used in a number of settings associated with the elementary teacher education program at our university. All involved groups in which the majority of the participants were white, female, over 30 years of age, better educated than the population in general, and middle class. All were invited--and some were assigned-- to use the intervention in settings of their own and to share their findings with us. As a result, a number of stories have been collected. They provide glimpses into the culture within which we work and suggest that hard questions interrupt complacency.

Gender bias exists in our minds. How do we eliminate it?

The eagerness of the graduate student who wrote this question to replicate the Cowgirls intervention was typical. It seemingly was taken both as a chance to explore gender bias issues as well as an opportunity to become more adept with inquiry. The intervention was replicated with fidelity in an undergraduate literacy methods class with 16 female students. After discussion the initial consensus was that gender bias is mostly dependent on traditional thinking and past living styles. Following their group investigations of children's literature, the students concluded that there is less gender bias in children's literature nowadays with more books emphasizing that girls can do the same jobs as boys can. They were, however, concerned that the sample of books they used was not large enough to reflect the actual situation in society. One shifted the responsibility from the author saying that gender bias sometimes results from the interpretation of the reader. At the end of the session in which they were faced with a public decision regarding the need for continuing concern about gender bias in children's literature, six students said there was no longer a need; two said there was; two students abstained; and six literally stood in the middle unable or unwilling to either support or reject the hypothesis.

I wonder if females are truly represented as heroes in the newer children's literature selections

Given the chance to study further the status of perceived gender bias in last years of the 20th Century, this inquirer chose to replicate the intervention with a group of advanced level tenth graders described as second-language learners of low socioeconomic status. The response of the class was surprising to the investigator: I thought they would laugh or react in a funny way, but actually their reaction was one of shock. Everyone got quiet when I read the last page. They said,

Lucky is a boy's name. There was no hair showing under the hat to show it was a girl. Only a boy would go to the rodeo and go down front with his father; a girl would sit in the stands with the grandmother and mother. Their results of their survey of children's books is predictable; they did not see anything out of order in any of the books. The investigator concluded: Culture may have something to do with the fact that they do not feel there is any gender bias in the books I took for them. They all pretty much agreed that there is a place for the male and female. They thought the main character being a girl strange.... I feel this tells us that our job of eliminating gender bias has not been completed. The final words in this story belong to the young man in this classroom where concerns for gender bias in children literature and perhaps also in society are less than apparent who wrote, Why should women not be able to do a man's job in the books?

What is wrong with gender bias in children's literature?

This questioner took the longest to complete the assigned replication and developed the most original adaptation--and least faithful replication--of the design. Sixteen second graders (7 boys and 9 girls) wrote names in blanks in each of five sentences about occupations such as nurse and scientist. Then they heard White Lightning and Curly Kidd and had the chance to write their hard questions. Discussion of the names given served as scaffolding to the issue of gender bias and gave clues about the child's perceptions of gender and work roles. A simple analysis showed that twelve (4 boys and 8 girls) gave the teacher a female name; four a male name. Although all the boys gave the scientist a male name which suggests that role stereotypes still linger in this second grade class; a strong majority of the girls, eight, chose a female name. Although the students' questions suggested that they had not quite understood their task, one insightfully wrote, I thought that a girl was a boy. What did you think?

What is it all about and do nearly all books have it?

A seventh grader wrote this question as part of a class inquiry. Nineteen students--seven girls and twelve boys--first wrote their questions and then searched children's literature for evidence to support or reject a gender bias hypothesis. These students working easily in groups previously assigned by their teacher concluded that gender bias was highly evident in children's literature with the girls splitting nearly evenly at four and three, while the boys were nine to three. Two respondents used similar evidence to support a somewhat different point of view. One said, I feel that it is [gender biased], especially in fairy tales that are dealing with rescues and royalty. The man almost always fights the dragon and rescues the princess, and she is always the "helpless little victim" who is saved. I personally feel this should change. Another said, No, not all children's books contain gender bias. Most stories that do contain gender bias are about princesses and princes and things like that.

Did you find the teaching strategy [group inquiry] effective?

This question was among the modifications made by a graduate student in using the intervention with 21 academically talented seventh graders. Student involvement in discussion was high. Each student took responsibility for completing a book in a discussion with some groups completing as many as six books in the time allowed. The group as a whole was evenly divided on the issue of gender bias with ten choosing each side and one saying, sometimes. When analyzed by gender; however, differences were apparent. The strong majority of the girls--eight to five--said that children's literature is gender biased; while by a five to two majority, the boys expressed the opposite viewpoint. In contrast, they were unanimous in their appreciation for this method of working saying: Yes, because we had just a certain time to do everything, and we weren't just sitting in a desk listening to a teacher. We, also, got to have our own opinion. Yes, I enjoyed this because it gave me a chance to decide for myself if the literature we read is gender biased or not. Yes, because I never knew what it [gender bias] was, and it was fun reading the books I read as a child. Also, I liked getting into groups. Yes!!! We expressed our ideas and heard the ideas of our friends. This made us think differently.

Conclusion

We will continue our practice of education in a university, which is not much different than it was in the early 1960s before the civil rights and women's movements. We will seek to facilitate the formation of the critical mass necessary to effect institutional change in the direction of a woman-centered university. We will strive to create an awareness of persisting inequities by inviting hard questions and guiding inquiries to generate further questions because we believe that questions are more troubling than answers.

Notes

1. Stanford, B. H. 1992. "Gender Equity in the Classroom." In *Common Bonds: Anti-Bias Teaching in a Diverse Society*. eds., D. A. Byrnes and G. Kiger. Wheaton, MD: Association of Childhood Education International.

2. Bailey, B. L,, K. Scantlebury, and W. J. Letts. "Its Not My Style: Using Disclaimers to Ignore Gender Issues in Science." *Journal of Teacher Education* 48(1): 29-36.

3. Sadker, M. and David Sadker. 1986. "Sexism in the Classroom: From Grade School to Graduate School." *Phi Delta Kappan* 67(6): 513.

A modified version of this chapter will appear in *Childhood Education*, Vol 76, forthcoming.

Chapter 8

Recognizing Our Students: Enhancing Inclusion in the Psychology Curriculum

Margaret E. Madden

While a number of women psychologists contributed visionary work throughout the century, significant attention to women and gender issues in the psychology curriculum began about thirty years ago when the first psychology of women courses were developed and a broader range of researchers started to attend to matters of concern to women (O'Connell and Russo 1990, 1991). Feminist psychologists began to have a stronger organized voice in the field when pioneers established committees and divisions within professional organizations and separate organizations focusing on what was then labeled the psychology of women (Mednick and Urbanski 1991; Tiefer 1991). Although there is plenty of room for development in the field, the discipline has been transformed in many ways by the presence of teachers, scholars, and practitioners interested in gender issues (O'Connell and Russo 1991). Unfortunately, one of the areas in which further improvement is necessary is inclusiveness in curricula across the discipline, from introductory undergraduate courses to graduate and postdoctoral training.

The Invisibility of Women in Psychology Curricula

While an enormous amount of research in psychology considers gender issues and issues of particular importance to women (Madden and Russo 1997), many studies have documented the still disappointing representation of women in the curriculum, frequently through the examination of the textbooks relied upon so heavily by undergraduate instructors. Research on women and gender and, feminist analyses of important issues are still not yet well represented in introductory, developmental, social, abnormal, experimental, statistics, and special education textbooks (Bronstein and Palud 1988; Conti and Kimmel 1993; Denmark 1994; Foley and Safran 1994; Foster and Ianaccone 1994; Hogben and Waterman 1997; Lott 1988; Marecek 1993; Peterson and Kroner 1992). Although women's concerns are mentioned more frequently in textbooks than in the past, the discussions are often superficial and fail to recognize the important theoretical work of feminist psychologists. For example, coverage of feminism and sexism is negligible in introductory psychology textbooks (Hogben and Waterman 1997).

Furthermore, the representation of diverse women and their concerns are woefully inadequate. While more research attention has been directed towards ethnic groups in recent years, there has been only a modest increase in work examining both gender and ethnicity as important social identities for women (Madden and Hyde 1998). In textbooks, women of Color are virtually invisible: when women are represented they tend to be White; when members of ethnic minorities are included, they tend to be male. One study found that the life experiences of women of Color were mentioned only four times in the eleven textbooks surveyed for the research (Conti and Kimmel 1993). One examination of introductory textbooks found that racial minorities were underrepresented in pictures (Gay 1988). Another study of introductory textbook photographs reported that Native Americans are virtually absent, while Latinas were underrepresented and Asians overrepresented compared to their proportion in the U. S. population (Hogben and Waterman 1997). Examining the dominance cues in pictures with pairs of people, Hogben and Waterman (1997) also found that males were portrayed in positions indicating higher status than females in all ethnic groups.

Inclusion of members of underrepresented categories beyond gender and ethnicity is so rare that content analyses intended to examine them have been abandoned. For instance, portrayal of people with disabilities in introductory texts is so infrequent that meaningful analysis is impossible, though the absence itself is noteworthy (Hogben and Waterman 1997). Textbooks have inadequate and segregated treatment of issues of importance to lesbian, gay male, and bisexual individuals, as well (Simoni 1996). Even psychology of women curricula, which generally embrace the value of inclusiveness, have failed to adequately represent women's diverse experiences of ethnicity (Santos de Barona and Reid 1992), sexual orientation (Simoni 1996), or disability (Fine and Asch). Thus, while recognition of gender issues in the psychology curriculum has increased, there is still ample distance to cover to make the curriculum even marginally representative of diverse women's experiences.

Benefits to Students of Representation

Psychological literature demonstrates that students benefit from a curriculum that includes issues of importance to them as individuals and members of groups, thereby demonstrating the relevance of material to them. Relevance promotes learning, particularly among students for whom the academic discourse is foreign or cognitive development is quite concrete, most undergraduates by some accounts (Belenky et al., 1986; McKeachie 1986; Perry 1981). Students whose experiences as women, ethnic minorities, lesbians, or other underrepresented social identities will have difficulty applying course materials to their own lives or otherwise engaging in it (Chin and Russo 1998; Greene and Sanchez-Hucles 1998; Kimmel and Worell 1998).

Furthermore, inclusiveness promotes tolerance of difference and a learning environment that is comfortable for groups that have been invisible in the curriculum. Invisibility implies unworthiness and implicitly condones pervasive negative stereotypes (Brown 1989; Fine and Asch 1988; Hogben and Waterman 1997; Reid 1993; Roy 1993). However, merely mentioning categories does not automatically promote tolerance. Indeed, in psychology gender differences have frequently been used to support derogatory stereotypes about women (Eagly 1987; Gilligan 1982; Lakoff 1973; Shields 1975), just as ethnic group differences and cross-cultural research have been used to justify racist practices (Goldstein 1995; Kamin 1974). If the behavior of White males is regarded as normative, then any group that behaves differently is treated as abnormal (Herrnstein and Murray 1994;

Caplan and Caplan 1994).   Many theorists have noted that the methodology of hypothesis testing has encouraged dichotomous comparisons of groups, thereby promoting normative comparisons (Kahn and Yoder 1989; Landrine et al., 1995; Sterling et al., 1995). Feminist psychologists have explored ways to talk about diversity without implying male or White superiority (Ginorio 1998; Weber 1998). Hence, how we study, understand, talk about, and interpret difference is as important for promoting tolerance as is including diverse groups.

Benefits of Inclusion for Psychology and Society

The field of psychology is being transformed by efforts to include women and other underrepresented groups in research, teaching, and practice.   Research considers issues that are important to women, reflect their typical experiences, or explore how gender and associated variables such as power, economic status, and family roles, affect women and men's psychological well-being (Madden and Russo 1997).   Incorporating this material into the curriculum not only engages students' interest, but also transforms the field.

Students who think they are not welcome in the academic community of psychology because they see no others who resemble them may pursue other fields (Gratch et al., 1995).   Students whose experiences lead them to behave differently from overrepresented groups may be explicitly or implicitly discouraged by possible mentors from pursuing work in the discipline, thereby magnifying underrepresentation.

Because psychologists bring their biased perspectives in defining what is worthy of investigation (Eagly and Carli 1981; Gannon et al., 1992), participation by researchers who are members of underrepresented groups increases the probability that questions defined by varied experiences will be considered important enough to study. For example, increased attention to women's experiences has promoted a vast amount of research on the origins and treatment of sexual abuse and domestic violence because these are experiences predominantly of women, though by no means exclusively (Burgess and Holmstrom 1979; Koss et al., 1994; Walker 1979).   Until women's voices were heard in the field, important questions about these issues were not even asked.

Research on gender and feminist theory has enhanced the understanding of the role of psychological theory (Fine and Gordon 1989; Hare-Mustin and Marecek 1988; Worell and Etaugh 1994), and critiques of conventional methodology have encouraged exploration of alternative ways to study human behavior (Denmark et al., 1988; Fine and Gordon 1989; Grossman et al., 1988; Hyde 1994; Landrine et al., 1995; Marecek 1995; Worell and Robinson 1994). Basic issues are raised about the adequacy of theory, the validity of measurement instruments, and the replicability of well-established phenomena (Landrine et al., 1995; Lewin and Wild 1991).

For example, using labels from the terminology of hypothesis testing, Hare-Mustin and Marecek (1988) describe the limitations of biases in research and applied psychology that exaggerate both gender differences, *alpha biases*, and gender similarity or equality, *beta biases*. Alpha biases lead to an emphasis on gender differences and ignore the many realms of behavior in which females and males are similar. Cultural feminist approaches to psychology are controversial among feminist psychologists because they tend to imply an essential difference in the values on which women make decisions and act (e.g., Chodorow 1978; Gilligan 1982). On the other hand, recent critiques of feminist psychology have suggested that the beta bias, which emphasizes similarity and equality at the expense of genuine gender differences in character or experience, has become the dominant ideology of feminist psychology and silenced more realistic (Eagly 1995) or radical (Crowley-Long 1998) theoretical perspectives.

The psychology curriculum must reflect these transformations of the field. Students must learn to recognize dichotomous thinking, ignorant acceptance of positivist assumptions, methodologies that place excessive value on generalization to "all" people, and the advantage of using diverse methodologies to investigate phenomena. Yet research methods books rarely include these critiques and few graduate programs provide courses in qualitative or other forms of research (Caplan and Caplan 1994; Quina and Kulberg 1988). Teaching students to be more sophisticated consumers or producers of research will enhance both the discipline of psychology and the understanding in society of the impact of gender assumptions on everyday behavior and our understanding of it (Bohan 1997; Chin and Russo 1998; Santos de Barona and Reed 1992).

Not only has feminist theory influenced discussions about methodology in psychology, but it also has contributed to the broader discussion among scientists about assumptions inherent in the scientific method relied upon throughout the natural, physical, and social sciences. Research by psychologists substantiates claims by other scientists that lack of inclusiveness, biased metaphors and language, and pedagogical methods that exclude or alienate women and other minorities constrict theoretical thinking, impose unanalyzed assumptions, and otherwise limit the applicability or validity of scientific research (Fausto-Sterling 1997; Keller 1985; Rosser 1990; Schiebinger 1993).

Feminist psychologists are explicit in describing links among the political, professional, and private. Their critiques go beyond simply questioning the assumption that research, teaching, and practice are apolitical to explicitly valuing activist research that promotes the well-being of others, particularly women and others in lower status positions (Brabeck and Brown 1998; Greene and Sanchez-Hucles 1998; Grossman et al., 1998; Worell and Johnson 1998).

One important activist view is recognition that people who lack power often cope with their powerlessness in ways that may not be perceived as adaptive by others who do not understand the context of the situation, particularly the constrictions derived from lack of status. For example, feminist psychologists have pointed out that focusing on the question "why do they stay with their husbands?" about women in battering relationships fails to recognize the narrow range of options available to many women. Moreover, it fails to recognize the reality that physical risks may be greater for women who leave a battering relationship than those who stay, or that many women engage in numerous other actions that represent coping or survival tactics (Wyche and Rice 1998).

Difficulties of Promoting Inclusion

However much instructors value inclusiveness, implementing a representative curriculum is not easy and psychologists have begun to write about the difficulties encountered and suggest solutions for dealing with problems (Madden and Hyde 1998). In this section, I outline some of these problems and describe possible responses to them.

Discussing sensitive issues.

Frequently students and teachers find discussing race, sexuality, or ability very difficult. Discussing these topics may be embarrassing or considered impolite by some. Implicitly, at least, people of privileged status may not want to admit that privilege has afforded them opportunities that others lack or may feel it is rude to flaunt their status (Greene and Sanchez-Hucles 1998; McIntosh 1993). Even well intentioned individuals may not have the language or experience to discuss such issues or may worry about offending others or being perceived as one of the enemy. Focusing on primary sources and psychological theory and research can sometimes provide the vehicle to engage in those conversations in less threatening and personal ways (Simoni 1996), avoiding disclosure of personal experiences or beliefs beyond a comfortable level.

The tendency of psychology to focus on differences between groups contributes to a reluctance to discuss race at all. As recent initiatives regarding race relations in the United States acknowledge, Americans seem to have difficulty talking about race, and many of us probably feel this in our classrooms (Cose 1996). Pedagogical approaches that give us a language to discuss race may help reduce discomfort and allow students to listen to one another. The discussion should focus on how people's experiences may be affected by their race, rather than perpetuating the notion that race or ethnicity "causes" predetermined personality and behavioral tendencies (Ginorio and Martinez 1998; Okazaki 1998; Weber 1998).

In her article about gender issues in Asian American psychology, Okazaki (1998) says:

> It is far more informative to ask "What is it about being Asian American that is producing this effect on variable X?" than to ask, for example, "Do Asian Americans and non-Asian Americans differ on variable X (p. 36)."

She cites gender stereotypes of Asian Americans and pressures to assimilate to the American ideal as among factors that may affect psychological variables such as self-concept and self-esteem.

Writing about Latinas, Ginorio and Martinez (1998) argue that ethno-racial identity is foregrounded for members of minority groups because of power differentials that are completely confounding of ethno-racial category, even within broad groupings such as Hispanic American. Other variables linked correlationally with ethnicity are level of acculturation, socioeconomic status, language fluency, affectional and sexual orientation, and motivational issues related to educational achievement, and, of course, gender role socialization.

Classroom exercises and assignments can also provide a vehicle to discuss these matters in ways that are less likely to provoke defensiveness. Ginorio (1998) describes a class on violence in which students role-played a social identity different from their own and attempted to interpret class material from the vantage of that identity. Assuming the viewpoint of that identity required examining other variables related to the category, promoting the more sophisticated analysis these complex interactions require.

Authority and expertise.

Questions of authority and expertise pose paradoxes that sometimes create no-win situations for instructors. On one hand, there are many compelling arguments supporting the notion that research in psychology would be more representative of the experiences of underrepresented groups if members of those groups are among the researchers at the table (Reid 1993; Reid and Kelly 1994; Task Force on Representation in the Curriculum, 1995). On the other hand, instructors who teach about groups to which they belong (other than White males) are often perceived as biased. Moore and Trahan (1997) report that students rated syllabi for courses about gender as more biased and political when they were purported to have been written by female instructors than when they were supposedly by male instructors. Others report anecdotally that students seem to overestimate the attention paid to ordinarily neglected topics, as Simoni (1996) notes about attempts to include issues of important to lesbians and gay men.

One strategy to enhance authority is to rely on the voluminous scholarly psychological literature on diverse women to support claims that might otherwise be perceived as political. Yet one must also acknowledge the limits of traditional positivist research methodologies and avoid undermining the legitimacy of the varied individual experiences of students. As with research, instructors' awareness and acknowledgment of their own biases is vital. However, even recognition of those assumptions must be presented in such a way that students understand that other instructors who pretend to portray value-free instruction are also biased and perhaps more insidious in not admitting or understanding their own assumptions.

Complexity of interactions

Psychological research, with its emphasis on identifying causal relationships using controlled experimental design, often focuses on a few variables simultaneously, therefore examining gender without assessing other subject characteristics such as ethnicity, or contextual features, such as power, that interact with gender. Certainly complex interactions are more difficult to interpret and explain to most audiences, including undergraduates. Theoretical and pedagogical models which offer frameworks for interpreting complex interactions permit instructors to suggest complexity without requiring sophisticated understanding of multiple factors on the part of students (Ginorio and Martinez 1998; Okazaki 1998; Weber 1998).

Examining sociological and psychological literature on race, class, gender and sexuality, Weber (1998) describes six common themes: these categories are "[1] historically and [2] globally specific, [3] socially constructed [4] power relations that simultaneously operate on both [5] the macro (social) and [6] micro (individual) levels of society (p. 13)." Using these dimensions to discuss the intersection of these factors leads to a richer, more sophisticated understanding of their effect on psychological variables.

That psychology has largely ignored the importance of the differential power or status associated with gender and other variables has been noted often by feminist psychologists (Worell and Johnson 1998), neglect compounded by the tendency of psychological research to disregard the impact of context on behavior. Even social psychology, which explores contextual factors specifically, has tended to reduce those factors to one or two variables that can be manipulated in experimental designs, considerably diluting the impact of context (Milgram 1963). Collins (1998) describes a classroom exercise demonstrating the importance of power variables in psychopathology. After watching a video of Zimbardo's (Haney and Zimbardo 1977) well-known prison study, students rate the prisoners and guards and then examine parallels with roles seen in women and men therapy.

Along with analysis of power and status, an examination of concepts such as oppression, privilege, and meritocracy is important for both instructors and students. Greene and Sanchez-Hucles (1997) propose that all psychologists (teachers, researchers, and therapists) must understand these concepts before the discipline can be tolerant of diversity. Many instructors have found that McIntosh's (1993) discussion of White privilege is a potent tool for presenting these concepts in a way that helps students understand and accept the concept of privilege.

Volume of material

Every new teacher discovers immediately that there is too little time to cover everything she would like to cover in most courses, particularly undergraduate survey courses (McKeachie 1986). Now that there is substantial research on gender, women, ethnicity, and members of minority groups, how can one fit it into courses, particularly in areas of psychology with a long tradition and accepted canon of material?

Instructors must put this apparent glut of demands in focus: it has been a long time since one could cover all of most standards areas of psychology in one course and choices are always being made about what is important. Perhaps reliance on textbooks has encouraged a sense that there is certain material that one *must* cover. Explicit recognition that we have already made choices about what is important is a starting point, to be followed by careful assessment of the values implicit in those choices. Certainly my argument, and those of other authors in this volume, is that inclusiveness is sufficiently valuable to supersede other priorities. Convincing others in the academic community, such as textbook authors and test writers, is important, as well.

In addition, one can infuse course material with the discussion of gender and ethnicity in regard to other topics. Once again, frameworks for introducing concepts pertinent to diverse groups are helpful, using research on these groups to portray important theoretical constructs, rather than simply to describe a hodgepodge of experiences of people who happen to have different backgrounds (Ginorio 1998; Ginorio and Martinez 1998; Okazaki 1998; Weber 1998).

Include whom?

My experience parallels patterns of curricular transformation identified by various writers (Goldstein 1995; McIntosh 1983). It seems to be consistent with experiences of other instructors: my syllabi have evolved from complete lack of inclusion, to devoting a day to ethnic minority women or lesbians, to perhaps sprinkling research on these groups throughout the course, often to supplement textbooks that infrequently mention them. But this has never seemed like enough. In an attempt to represent the experience of all women, one ends up mentioning several token groups or lumping people with distinct national cultural heritages, such as Filipino Americans and Chinese Americans, into a meaningless heterogeneous group such as Asian Americans (Ginorio and Martinez 1998; Okazaki 1998; Weber 1998).

Psychologists have long questioned assumptions that gender differences are explained by biological differences and causes, yet we must also challenge the notion of race as a clearly delineated biological category. Neither race nor ethnicity is a distinctive variable that is helpful to understanding psychological matters. They contribute to social identity or political identity, but do not create identity themselves. Ethnicity often interacts with other variables in significant ways, *e. g.*, immigration, economic or educational status, or sexual orientation. Not only is ethnicity not a simple definitional category, but it is also not a very useful psychological one (Ginorio and Martinez 1998; Okazaki 1998; Weber 1998; Wyche 1998). Given that, the interaction of ethnicity with gender is difficult to unravel. Hence, one needs to consider alternative ways to define the groups we want to include in our courses, for instance by discussing ethnicity as a social or political identity instead (Ginorio and Martinez 1998; Okazaki 1998).

Difference schemas

The comparative nature of psychology continues to be a vexing problem, as much of the research tends to compare women with men or members of ethnic minority groups with the White majority culture. We need to develop strategies for dealing with difference as difference, not as evaluative comparison with some other group that may implicitly or explicitly be defined as the superior norm. There is a tension inherent in acknowledging within-group differences and allowing for discovery of experiences common to group members. When we discuss cultural norms that seem less egalitarian in gender roles in comparison to mainstream American culture, we run the risk of reinforcing inaccurate negative stereotypes (Goldstein 1995).

Goldstein (1995) suggests that cross-cultural research should be presented to students in a manner that encourages tolerance of difference, rather than promoting stereotypes. Instructors should avoid marginalization of cross-cultural materials and perspectives; discuss bias within cross-cultural literature; choose material that does not reinforce negative stereotypes; use accurate terminology to create cross-cultural comparison; distinguish between *emics*, culture-specific phenomena, and *etics*, phenomena that are universal across cultures; and create a classroom environment in which diversity is valued. These strategies also apply to the discussion of gender and ethno-race comparisons within American culture.

The discussion of gender roles within ethnic groups can be particularly problematic, because superficially some ethnic groups, for example Hispanics or Asian Americans, appear to hold more traditional or conservative values about gender roles than European Americans do. Several authors suggest ways to present cross-cultural gender issues without reinforcing the idea that mainstream culture automatically is more enlightened about gender issues (Ginorio and Martinez 1998; Okazaki 1998). For example, the process of migration, immigration status, and acculturation are some factors which research suggests affect gender role socialization of Latinas and vary among Hispanic groups from different countries of origin (Ginorio and Martinez 1998). Okazaki (1998) reports that students sometimes find the gender roles of Asians to be disturbing, alien, or immoral and, therefore, she encourages students to explore their own reactions to them. Instructors should point out that sexism still exists in mainstream American culture and that very traditional notions of gender roles dominated that culture very recently. She also suggests explicit and sophisticated discussion of cultural relativism and reasons for judgments of other cultures. Finally, she says it is crucial to examine the ethnic and sociocultural variation among members of Asian and Asian American cultures to avoid overgeneralizing differences identified by research.

On a more theoretical note, Crowley-Long (1998) argues that the liberal feminist bias in psychology of women texts, intent on proving the absence of difference between women and men, discourages inclusion of marginalized groups. Greater inclusion of socialist and radical feminist theoretical perspectives would promote representation within the discipline.

Interdisciplinary sources

Psychology has tended to be insulated from work in other disciplines. Yet, other disciplines have explored the construction of gender, race, and identity, psychologists should take advantage of interdisciplinary literature. However, instructors must deliberately seek to understand modes of discourse in other disciplines. Models of courses that use material from diverse sources are also available (Bohan 1997; Ginorio 1998; Ginorio and Martinez 1998; Okazaki 1998; Task Force on Representation in the Curriculum 1995; Weber 1998; Wyche 1998).

Conclusion

The task of representing women of diverse backgrounds and feminist psychological ideas in the curriculum is a broad one, as this discussion of some of the difficulties encountered by instructors demonstrates. However, numerous resources are available in the form of a vast amount of research on gender and women's issues, an increasing amount on women of varied ethnic backgrounds, and articles and other written material on specific courses and curriculum transformation in general.

At the first National Conference on Education and Training in Feminist Practice in 1993, a working group on curriculum transformation developed eight principles for developing and evaluating a feminist psychology curriculum (Chin and Russo 1997). As educators continue to attempt to transform the curricula of their courses, programs, and disciplines, keeping these values in mind is helpful for identifying priorities:

    Diversity
    Egalitarianism and empowerment
    Self-determination
    Complexity of psychological phenomena
    Connection among humans
    Social action

Self-reflection
Integrative perspectives

Many of the works cited in this chapter provide examples of curriculum content fulfilling these values. Chin and Russo (1997) reflect on the potential impact of each of these values on the psychology curriculum and suggest numerous other resources to facilitate curriculum transformation at the high school, undergraduate, graduate, and postgraduate levels. In addition, other collections and essays on transforming curricula in diverse areas of psychology are available (Bronstein and Quina 1988; Kimmel and Worell 1998; Landrine 1995; Madden and Hyde 1998; Madden and Russo 1998; McIntosh 1983; Task Force on Representation in the Curriculum, 1995). The task may be daunting and the goals not yet achieved, but ample resources are available to help instructors who wish to participate in this exciting transformation of psychology.

Chapter 9

Bringing Women's Ways of Knowing to Doctoral Research

Sharon Shelton-Colangelo and Lynn Becker Haber

While progressive teacher education programs often promote collaboration among graduate students, encouraging them to employ collaborative teaching and learning methodologies in elementary and secondary settings, this dedication to cooperative learning rarely extends to doctoral dissertation work.   Ironically, doctoral students who have read about, discussed, and enacted constructivist theories in their courses, for their culminating research too often must isolate themselves with their computers in a form of writing that has remained basically unchanged for centuries.

Successful completion of a dissertation in an institute of higher learning can be an admission ticket to academic jobs and privileges. Cooperation and collaboration directly challenge a narrative of power that has an elitist basis, designed as much to keep some people out of the academy as it is to open the doors to others. Because this elitism directly contradicted the feminist and student-centered philosophy espoused by the authors, we joined together in the spring of 1993 to test the limits of doctoral collaboration in the English education program at New York University (NYU).

As feminists, we were aware that feminist scholars over the past three decades have stressed cooperative, collaborative, and joint authorship (Belenky et al.,Witherall and Noddings 1986), but it has only been recently that doctoral research itself has begun to challenge traditional male-dominated assumptions about how knowledge is produced. Although there has been long-standing resistance to collaborative forms of education, we thought that this resistance comes out of outdated, rigid, unquestioned beliefs about learning that promote individualism and competitiveness. In our experience, we and many other women had found that our most positive and transformative learning took place in collaborative and cooperative settings. Furthermore, we wanted to challenge the notion that such learning should be relegated to forms that are considered less "scholarly" than doctoral research.

Our research plan was actually born much earlier during a NYU program at Oxford University. In the summer of 1991, as part of a class project at Oxford, we interviewed teachers participating in the program about their early experiences as students in elementary and secondary schools. We were interested in finding out how the autobiographical stories of these teachers were informing their constructs of teaching and further how reflecting on these stories might lead to progressive change in their constructs and in their practice. Through the course of the project, it became increasingly clear to each of us that we wanted to focus our dissertations on the role of such autobiographical reflection in bringing about teacher change. We realized that we learned more through our joint work than had we each carried out projects of our own, so we decided that we would like to work together on our doctoral research.

Our decision to pursue this form of collaboration was strongly influenced by the NYU English education program's emphasis on socially constructed knowledge and collaborative forms of learning. Not only were we affected by our professors' encouragement to collaborate on classroom projects, but we took to heart the stated philosophy of our program, which was included in the English education guide for doctoral and sixth year students. As the English education faculty states in this guide, "We even encourage dissertations done in tandem where, for example, two students analyze the same data in different ways. Our goal is to create a community of learners beginning with the opening sequence of doctoral seminars and lasting long after graduation."

Despite our program's emphasis on collaborative work in graduate courses and its suggestion that even collaboration on the dissertation research itself was permissible, we were pioneers in our efforts. We originally envisioned writing one collaborative document. In consultation with our committee, however, we decided to join together to design the study, gather our research, and engage in collaborative talk to help each other in the analysis of the data. We even ended up writing portions of our introductions and our entire methods section jointly, sharing our committee, and having joint defenses.   To our knowledge, no other dissertations at NYU had involved collaboration to this extent.   While we were disappointed that we would not be collaborating fully on our work, we were encouraged that we had pushed existing limits and were preparing the way for others who wished to go further in challenging the individualistic basis of the dissertation process.

As teacher educators dedicated to encouraging cooperation and sharing among our students, we felt strongly that we wanted to enact our own commitment to this kind of sharing on a doctoral level. Working together on the research for our dissertation represented our attempt to liberate ourselves from the widespread assumption that ideas are private property, that students learn best in isolation, and that the aim of education is to break students of their interdependencies with other selves for knowledge.   Our shared interest in teachers' early school autobiographies and our firm commitment to collaborative forms of learning brought us together in our search for deeper understandings of the stories which influence and shape teachers' teaching and learning lives.

Out of a desire to draw attention to the too often hidden collaboration in traditional research, we called our particular form of working together "Interdependent Feminist Inquiry."   This conception of collaboration   went   beyond   plural   authorship.   We   used "interdependent" as opposed to "dependent" or "independent" to suggest the reciprocal growth that accompanied our collaboration. In other words, as we discussed the meanings arising out of our participants' stories, we found that we built on and amplified each other's ideas. We purposely referred to our method as being feminist because we believed that collaboration, though not limited to women, could be considered a "women's way of knowing" that too often has been excluded from Western male-dominated learning institutions. In using the term "inquiry," we wanted to acknowledge the importance of critical questioning in the construction of knowledge. This term also suggested that our ideas, though informed by a definite philosophy, were not absolute principles but interpretations that were continually subject to revision.

According to Patti Lather, we are currently "in a period of dramatic shift in our understanding of scientific inquiry" from traditional quantitative methods that arose out of Enlightenment notions of "objective and absolute truth" and toward the progressive, hermeneutic, social constructivist framework that we believe qualitative research embraces. Thus we chose to engage in a qualitative study because we felt that it would give us a closer look at the people we researched than traditional quantitative methods might. We knew that qualitative research allowed participants to speak for themselves and to be authorities on their own lives. Moreover, it allows researchers and subjects to acknowledge emotion and to put personal knowledge at the center of the inquiry. It frankly admits the researcher, or researchers in this case, into the equation, and can often be transformative for all concerned.

According to   Bogdan and Biklen, Ely, and others, the term "qualitative research" may cover a vast range of methodologies, including naturalistic research, ethnographies, interpretative research, etc., what links these approaches is a common view that puts events in a social context, focuses on individuals, lets subjects speak for themselves, uses heavy description, and includes both intellect and emotion. These features appealed to us and constituted part of our decision to carry out this kind of research.

Two-with-one conversational interviews

The format we chose for our interviews was the one we used in Oxford, which involved a dynamic that we called "two with one" as opposed to "two against one." This approach was aimed at welcoming the participant into our collaboration. We saw this process as paralleling the potential that team teaching offers. Specifically, instead of increasing the disproportionate power of teachers over students, team teaching can diffuse singular power in a classroom by allowing students to see there might be many viewpoints held by teachers, that there is no one right way to act or think. Likewise, with our two-with-one interviews, we tried to consciously break down the disproportionate power between researcher and researchee, encouraging us all to collaborate and to learn together.

Open-ended personal interviews allowed us to enter into other people's constructs and to understand how their stories shaped them as teachers and learners. Such an attempt to enter into the thinking of others is central to George Kelly's personal construct theory, which recognizes that learning cannot take place when personal constructs, personal belief systems, are too rigidly in place to admit the possibility of change. Although we did not want to deny the importance of the value system by which we live and understand our lives, we nevertheless wanted to be flexible and to try to enter other peoples' ways of understanding in order to avoid stereotyping them, to learn, and to grow. Thus we conducted what Shulamit Reinharz describes as "conversational interviews." This term, which she says refers to an extremely "open-ended interviewee-guided investigation of a lived experience", seems to best characterize the kind of relationship we established with our participants.

An important practice cited by Reinharz involves the conscious effort on the part of some feminist researchers to strive for intimacy and trust between the researcher and the subject of research as an alternative to the traditional "scientific detachment" of the quantitative researcher. Embracing this philosophy, we approached the interviews with a strong desire to develop a trusting relationship with our participants. In order to do this, we found it was necessary to actively listen, that is, to listen and draw out interviewees on the basis of close attention to what they had to say. The Oxford experience was a crucial one because it enabled us to see how important it was to temporarily suspend judgment, to be empathic, to use tentative language, to try not to interrupt, and to offer encouragement and support as we asked those we interviewed to share their personal experiences. For example, when one of our Oxford participants told us about his rebellious behavior and boredom in his early school years, we attempted to actively listen by asking him to reflect on how his negative experiences in school influenced the way he approached his teaching. Because our question was inviting rather than judgmental, our interviewee had the opportunity to discover the important relationship between his early school boredom and his desire to be an entertainer with his own students. We felt that the context of the interview, which included many supportive responses such as probing questions and affirmative nods, gave him a safety net to make that discovery.

We believed that through active listening and sharing our genuine interest in the stories of our participants, we were able to create some sense of trust with everyone in the study. With some participants, we quickly developed close relationships while with others, it took more time to establish trust. Also although it was not our intent to act as therapists, we were struck by the fact that four out of six of our participants mentioned that the interviews felt a lot like therapy.

Collaborative data analysis

Although we discovered that our collaboration often required intensive effort, negotiation, and critical self-reflection, we knew that such an approach broadened our individual perspectives and allowed us to utilize our discussion with one another in constructing knowledge as we analyzed our data. Barnes among others has emphasized the importance of exploratory discussion in learning. Noting that the learning process involves the modification of our interpretative systems based on communication with other people, he states:

> In this book I call this groping towards a meaning 'exploratory talk'. It is usually marked by frequent hesitations, rephrasings, false starts and changes of direction. I want to argue that it is very important whenever we want the learner to take an active part in learning, and to bring what he learns into interaction with that view of the world on which his actions are based. That is, such exploratory talk is one means by which the assimilation and accommodation of new knowledge to the old is carried out. (28)

In line with Barnes' observations, we learned from communicating with one another and attempting to make sense of our data. We in fact considered each other's experiences and understandings to have been as valuable as the texts we consulted. In addition, the activity of articulating our own ideas helped us define and reflect on those ideas and subject them to critical scrutiny. This is a characteristic of speech that Barnes has observed:

> Speech, while not identical with thought, provides a means of reflecting upon thought processes, and controlling them. Language allows one to consider not only what one knows but how one knows it, to consider, that is, the strategies by which one is manipulating the knowledge, and therefore to match the strategies more closely to the problem. (98)

Thus the collaboration offered us the benefit of close social interaction with the possibility of continuous testing and extension of our ideas. We found that especially as we began our analysis of the data in our dissertations, our exploratory discussions proved very valuable in allowing us to temporarily suspend our own constructs and biases and to see through the eyes of another, which yielded a richer view of our participants' lives.

Furthermore, it was helpful for each of us to be able to consult with someone who had a unique "insider-outsider" perspective. That is, whenever one of us served as a consultant for the other, we were able to have both the familiarity with the data that arose from participating in the interviews and at the same time, to have the distance from the analysis that is needed to serve as a kind of audience. As consultants, we both developed common research questions and helped each other identify questions relating to our particular interests. We also shared the themes we elicited from the data and aided each other in expanding, refining, and revising these specific themes.

Working together allowed us not only to actively contest the traditional devaluation of collaborative educational experiences, but to acknowledge the importance of sharing multiple perspectives in the construction of knowledge. We openly and consciously became involved in analyzing the data that was used in each of our dissertations. In this phase of our collaboration, we were influenced by Mikhail Bakhtin's view that:

> As a living socio-ideological concrete thing, as heteroglot opinion, language for the individual consciousness, lies on the borderline between oneself and the other. The word in language is half someone else's. It becomes 'one's own' only when the speaker populates it with his own intention, his own accent, when he appropriates the word, adapting it to his own semantic and expressive intention. Prior to this moment of appropriation, the word does not exist in a neutral and impersonal language (it is not, after all, out of a dictionary that the speaker gets his words!), but rather it exists in other people's mouths, in other people's contexts, serving other people's intentions: it is from there that one must take the word, and make it one's own (293-294).

In working together to analyze our data, we openly acknowledged the influences of a wide range of others in constructing our ideas. As we had written elsewhere, we believed "that there are many unacknowledged voices that join together as we construct knowledge and express it. We consider collaboration rather than isolation, connectedness rather than separation, as key factors in learning" (Becker, Mancuso, Shelton-Colangelo 1993). We knew that too little attention had been paid to the collaboration inherent in all writing and thinking and, that hidden collaboration in academic research had taken many forms from informal discussions with members of the learning community to outright participation by others in one form or another in the writing.

Collaboration with participants

We also sought to collaborate with our participants in analyzing the data, basing our efforts on Lather's notion of reciprocity which "implies give-and-take, a mutual negotiation of meaning and power".   After each interview, we provided our participants with a copy of the previous conversation and invited comments and reflections. Moreover, not only did we as researchers discuss with each other the meanings we saw arising out of the interviews, but we also discussed with the interviewees their interpretations of their stories. For example, we sometimes paraphrased what we thought our participants were saying about their stories and asked them to respond.   Although occasionally our interpretations differed somewhat from those of the participants, their responses helped us make meaning out of the data and sometimes led us to change our interpretations.

Also both of us wrote letters to each of our participants in which we shared our preliminary interpretations of the data with them.   In each case, we read our letters aloud at the beginning of our third interview so that the participant could respond to our analysis and address possible misunderstandings and answer any further questions. We viewed these letters as important ways for us to give feedback to those involved in our study, to demystify our role as researchers, and to assure that the participants would have some idea of what we would be writing about them.

Because we had asked our participants to tell us personal stories about their educational backgrounds, we believed that we needed to reveal something about our own experiences in school. At the end of the interview period, we had a final informal dinner in which our participants met one another and shared their experiences so that they could get a better view of the entire study. It was at this dinner that the authors shared our own school stories with our participants and invited them to reflect on their implications for teaching and learning.

Writing up the data

Our collaboration was not over with the end of the interviews. Even though each of us wrote separate dissertations, we both continually functioned as a support system for the other and as consultants for developing and enriching the ideas and structures of our dissertations. As sources of support and solidarity, we went beyond what most doctoral support groups could provide since each of us had a strong investment in the other's study. We believed that this investment was a direct result of our collaboration in the development of the overall idea for the study, our active participation in all of the interviews, and our efforts to write up our findings. While we had divided the data so that each of us would write up only three of our six participants' stories, we both became closely acquainted with the life histories of all of them and continued to discuss the meanings of their early stories well into the writing period.

Our relationship as consultants for each other was a special one. As we began to write, we continued to talk, check our ideas, give each other feedback, provide critical questioning, and offer each other affirmation and encouragement. Although there were times when we had to negotiate decisions about our processes, we were guided by our shared belief in the importance of enacting progressive change in both schools and society. We often met to read each other's work and to talk about ways of strengthening our dissertations.

Working together as peers was empowering in many ways because we could try on new ideas in a relatively safe environment. In other words, our equal power relationship enabled us to function in much the same way as peer groups do in the classroom. We were able to push ideas to their limits and to take risks that we might not have taken otherwise. We found this willingness to take risks and freely explore ideas an important component in deepening our understandings.

As we wrote, we found that much of 'our' thinking went into each other's final dissertation product, because our view of writing itself was one that rejected the myth that ideas are totally original and belonging to one solitary individual. This is not to say that writers cannot bring different lenses to existing ideas or to construct new ones out of the social fabric of the old, but just that different lenses coming together can sometimes have more profound outcomes. In other words, there were times when our collaboration seemed to produce results far exceeding what each of us might do in isolation.

Shared orals

Our joint orals took place approximately four years after we had conceived our dissertation plans. At first our committee suggested that we divide the hearing into two segments, one for each of us to defend our research. After a few minutes with only one of us speaking, however, the committee decided that this division was artificial and that we both should just discuss our findings together. What occurred was an in-depth conversation involving us and our committee.   As had happened in the course of analyzing and writing up our research, one of us often found ourselves finishing the other's sentence. New ideas occurred to us as we talked. Committee members themselves joined in much the same spirit and later commented that the experience had been a powerful one for them as well.

The form of our orals directly challenged the medieval notion that doctoral hearings must be a lonely hazing ceremony for admission into the elite academy.   That there were two of us present changed the distribution of power relations at our final orals, making us more powerful and the discussion more egalitarian.   That is, instead of one student being questioned by a committee of gatekeepers, we all became interested in the ideas that the study raised and discussed them more as peers. Our hearing emerged as a group inquiry that seemed to empower all of us. It was both a learning experience and a celebration of our learning.

While we learned about the constructs of teaching of those we interviewed and the profound impact that autobiographical reflection can have on teachers' practice, we also learned about the value of collaboration on the dissertation level. Our insistence on pushing the collaboration as far as we could within the confines of our institution was based on a desire to unite our theory and practice by enacting our feminist beliefs. After the successful completion of our work, we were invited to the English education doctoral seminar to answer questions about our experience. We took this opportunity to encourage others to follow in our footsteps and to take our collaboration even further in the future.

If institutions of higher learning are truly to become more 'woman centered,' women's ways of thinking, speaking, and knowing need to be consciously incorporated at all levels. Transforming the doctoral experience to embrace collaborative dissertation writing, cooperation and reciprocity with research participants, and collaborative orals based on a conversation model instead of one resembling a fraternity hazing can go a long way in challenging the competition and adversarial discourse traditionally engendered within the academy.

Conclusion

Melanie McCoy and JoAnn DiGeorgio-Lutz

As the chapters in this volume indicate, the creation of a woman-centered university requires a university to both consciously and deliberately address educational equity for women as faculty, students, and administrators. Educational equity for women moves beyond equal treatment of women. It means equality of results. It means curricular justice. If a university education is structured so women are disadvantaged by their gender (gender refers to socially constructed roles ascribed to males and females which are learned, change over time and vary by culture) then women are restricted in their life aspirations and opportunities. A woman-centered university does not require a gender-free education but rather a gender-sensitive one. Barbara Houston states that the goal is not to ignore gender but rather to pay more attention to it.[1] As the chapters on women and pedagogy indicate, faculty need to inquire further into gender differences and not try to eradicate them. A gender-sensitive education can prevent sexual bias and sexual inequality.

Minnich states that equality and sameness are not identical.[2] To treat all students alike without recognizing differences is not equality. To include everybody would be to go for the lowest common denominator. It implies that to be different is to be inferior. Women students are the majority in higher education but are treated as a minority. White males are the minority but they continue to dominate university goals and values.

Knowledge is a human construct and it perpetuates and validates assumptions that are only recognized as assumptions when challenged. As Jones and Young contend, excellence and prejudicial elitism are not the same.[3] The university is a powerful tool for the dominant group in a given society because it reproduces cultural beliefs and economic relationships that support the elite group's privileges. Peggy McIntosh asserts, that to challenge the canon is to challenge Matthew Arnold's assertion that one subgroup in a society (Euro-males) can identify for all the best that has been thought and said in the world.[4] A curriculum that does not integrate material on women into courses suffers from gross scholarly inaccuracy and is historically inaccurate. All curricula are political and a curriculum that leaves out women and other outsider groups is highly politicized.

Margie Kitano asserts that one goal of public universities in the United States is to develop citizens for a democratic society.[5] This goal requires accurate, comprehensive disciplinary knowledge. It requires a pluralistic curriculum that promotes understanding of the contributions and perspectives of people of different genders, races, ethnic groups, cultures, languages, religions, and classes. A pluralistic curriculum broadens the world-view of students. It allows students to interact effectively with people different from themselves and prepares them to live in an increasingly interdependent world. A pluralistic curriculum acknowledges simultaneously the commonalties of human experiences and the differences that social and familial histories construct. This is what Rosenfelt describes as a "double consciousness," a tension between community and diversity.[6] The pluralistic curriculum provides students the knowledge they need to deal with an increasingly global economy and increasingly interconnected pattern of world affairs. The university is an important experiment in democracy. Negotiation of differences is a fact of public life, and trust and mutual respect is required in a democratic community.[7] The various chapters in this book have demonstrated that universities are indeed chilly places for women. In 1982, Roberta Hall and Bernice Sandler wrote *The Classroom Climate: A Chilly One for Women?*. With the publication of this work the term "chilly climate" entered the lexicon of higher education. The term is used to describe how the many small inequalities women students suffer can create a negative atmosphere for women students and women faculty members. In 1996, Bernice Sandler, Lisa Silverberg, and Roberta Hall published a new report, *The Chilly Classroom Climate, A Guide to Improve the Education of Women.* The new work was prompted by reports from women university students that their classroom experiences continue to be different from those of men and that these experiences continue to be unsatisfactory in ways that do not seem to be recognized by university faculty members and administrators.

A significant change that has occurred in the research literature since 1982, according to Sandler, Silverberg and Hall, is the attention now being paid to the intersection of gender with race, ethnicity, age, class, disabilities, religion and rural/urban differences. Most research in the past has looked at classroom behavior related to gender in a white, middle class environment. The differential treatment of women also happens to members of other outsider groups. Gender affects not only women. Race and ethnicity affect not only people of color. Men and whites are profoundly affected by their gender and race whether they are aware of it or not. Males pay a high price for being the preferred gender in the educational system just as whites do. For example, males grow up in U.S. society learning not to show emotion, to repress their feelings, to be aggressive, to compete, and to win. The end result is that: males often receive lower grades, are more likely to fail, are more likely to have trouble adjusting, are more likely to abuse alcohol and drugs, are more likely to commit suicide, and are more likely to feel like failures because of unrealistic career goals they feel compelled to pursue.

Twenty percent of the total U.S. population is racially and ethnically diverse. The 1990 census showed that 1 in 7 individuals speaks a language other than English at home.[8] Even though the concept of "multi-culturalism" or "cultural diversity" is given lip service in universities today, most universities are actually talking about inclusion of men of color, not women of color, into the curriculum. Even if universities are attempting to provide educational equity to women, they are usually referring to white, middle class women. Women do share many commonalties that emerge out of the shared experiences of being a woman and of societal treatment of women. However, women also differ in significant ways, for example age, class, race and ethnicity.[9]

To be effective, movement toward the creation of a woman-centered university must also include changes in the campus climate, including its culture, habits, decisions, practices and policies that make up campus life as perceived by the diverse members of the university community. A critical part of this "climate" is how diverse both the faculty and administration are at a given university. A diverse faculty and administration are critically important if the curriculum and other features of the university are to be transformed. Men comprise 68 percent of all higher education faculty members; whereas, women are 33 percent. Women faculty members outnumber men only at the lowest, entry level positions.   Twenty percent of the total U.S. population is racially and ethnically diverse compared to 11 percent of the faculty, of which, only 5 percent are women of color.   Who the faculty members are does make a significant difference in course content, pedagogy, job satisfaction, and preparation for tenure. Moreover, as the contributors to this work demonstrate, women's ability as faculty, students, and administrators, to maneuver within the institutional environment is a key factor in movement toward change.

Our assessment of the preceding chapters' responses to the central question we posed to all the contributors of this work—"if a university was to commit itself fully to provide women an equal education, what would it need to do and what barriers exist that prevent change in this direction?'—is a mixture of both optimism and despair.   Our discouragement centers around the institutional barriers that women faculty and administrators continue to routinely encounter within the academic milieu.   As Conway-Turner notes in chapter one, African American women are still hampered by the twin pillars of racism and sexism as they maneuver the university setting and attempt to establish themselves professionally by gaining tenure in a system "that was not designed to accommodate African American women".   In order to avoid prematurely dropping out of the system as many African American faculty are inclined to do as the tenure deadline approaches, Johnson provides many invaluable guidelines for African American women faculty such as networking, creating research dossiers, and establishing a mentor-type relationship within the individual's department.   Despite the obstacles that minority women faculty members face in institutions of higher learning, we found that Conway-Turner's field notes provided a measure of optimism to our query.   Many of her cogent observations not only serve women of color, but provide sound advice for all women faculty that transcends racial barriers.   The remaining chapters that addressed the status of women faculty and administrators also served to highlight the barriers that need to be bridged to create a woman-centered university.   While Firestone called our attention to the impact of perceptions and the relationship of gender to levels of job satisfaction in the university in chapter two, Miller, Miller, and Schroth tendered a model for gender equity and cultural justice in chapter three.   Arlton, Lewellen, and Grissett in chapter four, reminded us of the social constructs within particular systems that continue to act as psycho-social barriers hindering women's achievement and advancement as both administrators and faculty in academia, thus contributing to our overall discouragement for movement toward a women-centered university.

Our greatest reassurance, however, came from the chapters that were applied pedagogy. Not only were they applied in the sense that the contributors demonstrated how they warmed the chilly classroom climate for women by designing course strategies to actively include women and minorities present in the classroom setting, but they also incorporated women and gender into a curriculum not confined exclusively to the realm of gender studies. For example, DiGeorgio-Lutz includes women's issues in non-gender specific international relations courses while Johnson discusses how women's issues expand traditional understandings of the field of anthropology in Australia. Madden awakened us to the many reasons why diverse women are not generally included in the psychology curriculum. Madden observed that because diverse women, along with other racially different groups in society, are consistently compared to the dominant group, misperceptions as well as attitudes of defensiveness permeate the learning environment. Because most instructors would rather not address those attitudes in their classrooms, women and other minorities receive scant attention. Her observations note a variety of pedagogical approaches that allow instructors to diffuse the potential for defensiveness in classes where race and diversity are included in the psychology curriculum. Also, Foote and Walker gave us their perspective as instructors of future elementary education teachers, contributing to our insight regarding gender equity. Finally, Shelton-Colangelo and Becker Haber also renewed our faith in the potential for transformation of the university to reflect more gender equity with their discussion of the trials and tribulations they experienced writing a collaborative dissertation. The significance of their chapter underscores the role that women students can play in the creation of a woman-centered university. Lastly, despite the limitations and the small measures of success presented in this book, the preceding chapters, nonetheless, point to the need for an integrated approach to establishing gender equity within and among institutions of higher learning.

It is our hope that the preceding chapters serve to awaken and motivate others to recognize the importance of our call for institutional change in the direction of a woman-centered university that will serve to benefit all of humankind.

Notes

1. Houston, Barbara. 1996. "Gender Freedom and the Subtleties of Sexist Education." In *The Gender Question in Education*, eds., Ann Diller, Barbara Houston, Kathryn Pauly Morgan, and Maryann Ayim. Boulder, CO: Westview Press, 54-60.

2. Minnich, Elizabeth K. 1989. "From the Circle of the Elite to the World of the Whole: Education, Equality, and Excellence." In *Educating the Majority: Women Challenge Tradition in Higher Education*, eds., Carol S. Pearson, Donna L. Shavlik, and Judith G. Touchton. New York: Collier-Macmillan. 277-293.

3. Jones, Terry and Gale S. Young. 1997. "Classroom Dynamics: Disclosing the Hidden Curriculum." In *Multicultural Course Transformation in Higher Education*, eds., Ann Intili Morey and Margie Kitano. Boston, MA: Allyn and Bacon.

4. McIntosh, Peggy. 1989. "Curricular Re-vision: The New Knowledge for a New Age." In Pearson, et al., 400-412.

5. Kitano, Margie K. 1997. "A Rationale and Framework for Course Change." In Morey, et al.., 12.

6. Rosenfelt, Deborah S. 1997. "Doing Multiculturalism: Conceptualizing Curricular Change." In Morey, et al., 50.

7. Appel, Morgan, David Cartwright, Daryl G. Smith, and Lisa E. Wolf. 1997. *The Impact of Diversity on Students" Preliminary Review of the Research Literature*. Washington, D.C.: Association of American Colleges and Universities.

8. Lynch, Eleanor. 1997. "Instructional Strategies." In Morey, et al., 56-70.

9. Pearson, et al., 16.

Bibliography

Abu-Lughod, Lila. 1990. "The Romance of Resistance: Tracing
   Transformations of Power Through Bedouin Women." *American
   Ethnologist*, 17(1): 41-55.
Adelman, C. 1992. *Women at Thirtysomething: Paradoxes of
   Attainment*, 2nd ed., Office of Research, United States Department of
   Education.
Anzaldua, Gloria, and Cherrie Moraga, eds. 1981. *This Bridge
   Called My Back: Writings by Radical Women of Color.* CITY:
   Persephone Press.
American Association of University Professors (AAUP). 1996.
   "Annual Report on the Economic Status of the Profession."
   Washington, D. C..
Appel, Morgan, David Cartwright, Daryl G. Smith, and Lisa E. Wolf.
   1997. *The Impact of Diversity on Students: Preliminary Review of
   the Research Literature.* Washington, DC: Association of
   American Colleges and Universities.
Argyris, Chris. 1973. "Personality and Organization Theory
   Revisited." *Administrative Science Quarterly*, 18: 141-167.
Association of Professional Women at UT-Dallas 1995. "Summary
   Report: Why do Faculty Women Leave UT-Dallas?" Unpublished.
Bailey, B.L., K. Scantlebury, and W.J. Letts. "Its Not My Style:
   Using Disclaimers to Ignore Gender Issues in Science." *Journal of
   Teacher Education*, 48(1): 29-36.
Bakhtin, Mikhail. 1981. *The Dialogic Imagination.* Austin:
   University of Texas Press.
Banks, James A. 1988. "Approaches to Multicultural Curriculum
   Reform." *Multicultural Leader*. Spring. Edmonds, WA:
   Educational Materials and Services
Barnes, Douglas. 1992. *From Communication to Curriculum*.
   Portsmouth, NH: Boynton-Cook.

Bateson, Mary. 1994. *Peripheral Visions: Learning Along the Way.*
New York: Harper Collins.
Bauer, Dale M. and S. Jaret McKinstry, eds., 1991. *Feminism,
Bakhtin, and the Dialogic.* Albany, NY: State University Press.
Becker, Lynn, Carolina Mancuso, and Sharon Shelton-Coangelo.
1993. "The Connected Classroom: A Conversation on Feminist
Pedagogy." *Critical Issues,* 1: 1-22.
Beckman, Mary. 1991. "Feminist Teaching Methods and the Team-
Based Workplace: Do Results Match Intentions?". *Women's
Studies Quarterly,* 1&2: 165-178.
Begnal, Kate. 1991. "Knowing Difference: Internationalizing a
Women-and-Literature Course." *Women's Studies International
Forum,* 14(4): 285-294.
Belenky, Mary F., Blythe M. Clinchy, Nancy R. Goldberger, and Jill
M. Tarule. 1986. *Women's Ways of Knowing: The Development of
Self, Voice, and Mind.* New York: Basic Books.
Bender, Frederic L., ed., 1988. *The Communist Manifesto.* New
York: W. W. Norton and Company.
Benstock, Shari, ed., 1988. *The Private Self: Theory and Practice of
Women's Autobiographical Writings.* Chaper Hill, NC: University
of North Carolina Press.
Blauner, Robert. 1964. *Alienation and Freedom.* Chicago:
University of Chicago Press.
Blom, G., R. Waite, and S. Zimit. 1970. "Motivational Content
Analysis of Children's Primers." In *Basic Studies of Reading,* eds.,
H. Levin and J. Williams. New York: Basic Books.
Bogdon, Robert and Sari Biklen. 1982. *Qualitative Research for
Education: An Introduction to Theory and Methods.* Boston: Allyn
and Bacon.
Boice, R. 1993. Early Turning Points in Professional Careers of
Women and Minorities." In *New Directions for Teaching and
Learning.* No. 53. San Francisco: Jossey Bass Publishers.
Bonjean, Charles M., Billye J. Brown, Burke D. Grandjean, and
Partick O. Macken. 1982. "Increasing Work Satisfaction through
Organization Change: A Longitudinal Study of Nursing Educators."
Journal of Applied Behavioral Science, 18: 357-369.
Bohan, Janis S. 1997. "Teaching on the Edge: The Psychology of
Sexual Orientation." *Teaching of Psychology,* 24(1): 27-32.

Brabeck, Mary, and Laura Brown. 1998. "Feminist Theory and Psychological Practice." In *Shaping the Future of Feminist Psychology: Education, Research, and Practice*, eds., Judith Worell and Norine Johnson. Washington, D.C.: American Psychological Association.

Bronstein, Phyllis, and Michele Paludi. 1988. "The Introductory Psychology Course from a Broader Human Perspective.". In *Teaching a Psychology of People: Resources for Gender and Sociocultural Awareness*, eds., Phyllis Bronstein and Kathryn Quina. Washington, D.C.: American Psychological Association.

Bronstein, Phyllis, and K. Quina, eds. 1988. *Teaching a Psychology of People: Resources for Gender and Sociocultural Awareness.* Washington, D.C.: American Psychological Association.

Brown, Laura S. 1989. "New Voices, New Visions: Toward a Lesbian/gay Paradigm for Psychology." *Psychology of Women Quarterly,* 13(4): 445-58.

Burgess, A. W., and L. L. Holmstrom. 1979. "Adaptive Strategies and Recovery from Rape." *American Journal of Psychiatry,* 136: 1278-82.

Braverman, Harry. 1974. *Labor and Monopoly Capital.* New York: Monthly Review Press.

Breese, J. R. and R. O'Toole. 1995. "Self-Definition Among Women Students." *Journal of Research and Development in Education,* 29: 27-39.

Bretherton, Charlotte. 1996. "Global Environmental Politics: The Gendered Agenda." Paper presented at the annual meeting of the International Studies Association. San Diego, CA.

Britton, G. E., and M.C. Lumpkin. 1977. "For Sale: Subliminal Bias in Textbooks." *The Reading Teacher,* 31: 40-45.

Britton, J. 1972. *Language and Learning.* London: Pelican Books.

Brodzki, Bella, and Celeste Schenck. 1988. *Life/Lines: Theorizing Women's Autobiography.* Ithaca: Cornell University Press.

Bronstein, P, E. Rothblum, and S. Solomon. 1993. "Ivy Halls and Glass Walls: Barriers to Academic Careers for Women and Ethnic Minorities." In *New Directions for Teaching and Learning.* No. 53. San Francisco: Jossey Bass Publishers.

Bulkin, Elly, Minnie Bruce Pratt, Barbara Smith, eds. 1984. *Yours in Struggle: Three Feminist Perspectives on Anti-Semitism and Racism.* Ithaca: Firebrand.

Bunch, Charlotte. 1987. "Not by Degrees: Feminist Theory and Education." In *Passionate Politics: Essays 1968-1986.* New York: St. Martin's Press.

Butt, Richard, Danielle Raymond, G. McCue, and L. Yamagishi. "Collaborative Autobiography and the Teacher's Voice." In *Studying Teacher's Lives,* ed., Ivor Goodson. New York: Teachers College Press.

Campbell, P. 1986. "What's a Nice Girl Like You Doing In A Math Class?" *Phi Delta Kappan* 67(7): 516-520.

Caplan, Paula, and Jeremy Caplan. 1994. *Thinking Critically About Research on Sex and Gender.* New York: HarperCollins.

Carfagna, Rosemarie. "A Developmental Core Curriculum for Adult Women Learners." *Learning Environment for Women's Adult Development,* 54-58.

Chamberlain, M. K., ed., 1988. *Women in Academe: Progress and Prospects.* New York: Russell Sage Foundation.

Checkland, P. 1981. *Systems Thinking, Systems Practice.* New York: Wiley.

Chin, Jean Lau, and Nancy Felipe Russo. 1998. "Feminist Curriculum Development: Principles and Resources." In *Shaping the Future of Feminist Psychology: Education, Research, and Practice,* eds., Judith Worell and Norine Johnson. Washington, D.C.: American Psychological Association.

Chodorow, Nancy. 1978. "The Reproduction of Mothering." Berkeley: University of California Press.

Clague, M. W. 1992. "Hiring, Promoting, and Retaining African American Faculty: A Case Study of An Aspiring Multi-Cultural Research University." Paper presented to the Association for the Study of Higher Education, Minneapolis, Minnesota.

Clark, S.M., and M. Corcoran. 1986. "Perspectives on the Professional Socialization of Women Faculty: A Case of Accumulative Disadvantage?" *Journal of Higher Education,* 57: 20-43.

Clarkson, F. 1998. "Anti-Abortion Violence: Two Decades of Arson, Bombs, and Murder." *Intelligence Report,* 91: 13-16.

Clinchy, B. M., M. F. Belenky, N. Goldberger, and J. Tarule. 1985. "Connected Education for Women." *Journal of Education,* 167: 28-45.

Collins, Lynn H. 1998. "Illustrating Feminist Theory: Power and Psychopathology." *Psychology of Women Quarterly*, 22(1): 97-112.

Commission on the Status of Women. Report to the President, 1992-1993. University of Delaware.

Coulton, C. J., 1981. "Person-Environment Fit As The Focus In Health Care." *Social Work*, 26: 289-296.

Copenhaver, J. 1993. "Instances of Inquiry." *Primary Voices K-6*, 2(1): 6-14.

Cose, E. 1996. "Twelve Steps Toward Racial Harmony." *Newsweek* 128 (November 25): 54-55.

Crosby, Faye J. 1982. *Relative Deprivation and Working Women*. New York: Oxford University Press.

Crowley-Long, Kathleen. 1998. "Making Room for Many Feminisms: The Dominance of the Liberal Political Perspective in the Psychology of Women Course." *Psychology of Women Quarterly*, 22(1): 113-30.

Cusimano, Maryann K. 1995. "Why Do You Do What You Do the Way You Do It? Examining Teaching Goals and Teaching Methods." Department of Politics, The Catholic University of America, Washington, DC. http://csf.colorado.edu/CaseNet/

Darling-Hammond, L. 1996. "The Quiet Revolution: Rethinking Teacher Development." *Educational Leadership*, 53(6): 4-11.

Davis, Angela. 1981. *Women, Race and Class*. NY: Randon House.

DePree, Max. 1989. *Leadership is an Art*. NY: Dell Publishing.

Denmark, Florence L. 1994. "Engendering Psychology." *American Psychologist*, 49(4): 329-34.

Denmark, Florence, Nancy F. Russo, Irene H. Frieze, and Jeri A. Sechzer. 1988. "Guidelines for Avoiding Sexism in Psychological Research." *American Psychologist*, 43: 583-85.

Dever, Maryanne, ed., 1997. *Australia and Asia: Cultural Transactions*. Honolulu: University of Hawaii Press.

Diller, Ann, Barbara Houston, Kathy Morgan, and Maryann Ayim. 1996. *The Gender Question In Education: Theory, Pedagogy, and Politics*. Boulder, CO: Westview Press.

Donath, Jackie R. 1997. "The Humanities." *Multicultural Course Transformation in Higher Education*, eds., Ann Intili Morey and Margie K. Kitano. Boston: Allyn and Bacon.

Dunn, Kathleen. 1993. "Feminist Teaching: Who Are Your Students?" *Women's Studies Quarterly*, 3&4: 39-45.

Dziech, B.W. and L. Weiner. 1990. *The Lecherous Professor: Sexual Harassment on Campus*, 2nd ed., Chicago: University of Illinois Press.

Eagly, Alice H. 1987. *Sex Differences in Social Behavior: A Social-role Interpretation*. Hillsdale, NJ: L. Erlbaum.

------. 1995. "The Science and Politics of Comparing Women and Men." *American Psychologist*, 50:145-58.

Eagly, Alice H., and Linda L. Carli. 1981. "Sex of Researchers and Sex-typed Communications as Determinants of Sex Differences in Influenceability: A Meta-analysis of Social Influence Studies." *Psychological Bulletin*, 90: 1-20.

Ebert, Teresa. 1991. "The 'Difference' of Postmodern Feminism." *College English*, 53: 886-904.

Eccles, J. and P. Blumenfeld. 1985. "Classroom Experiences and Student Gender: Are There Differences and Do They Matter?" In *Gender Influences in Classroom Interaction*, eds., L.C. Wilkinson and C..B. Marett. Orlando, FL: Academic Press.

Engel, G. L., 1980. "The Clinical Application of the Bio-psychosocial Model." *American Journal of Psychiatry*, 137: 535-542.

El Saadawi, N. 1980. *The Hidden Face of Eve*. London: Zed Books.

Ely, Margot. 1991. *Doing Qualitative Research: Circles Within Circles*. New York: The Falmer Press.

Enloe, Cynthia. 1989. *Bananas, Beaches, and Bases: Making Feminist Sense of International Politics*. Berkeley: University of California Press.

Essed, Philomena. 1994. "Making and Breaking Ethnic Boundaries: Women's Studies, Diversity, and Racism." *Women's Studies Quarterly*, 3&4: 232-249.

Etaugh, Carol. 1984. "Women Faculty and Administrators in Higher Education: Changes in Their Status since 1972." *Journal of the National Association for Women Deans, Administrators, and Counselors*, Fall: 21-25.

Exum, W. H. 1983. "Climbing the Crystal Stair: Values, Affirmative Action, and Minority Faculty." *Social Problems*, 39: 383-99.

Farley, J. 1990. "Women Professors in USA: Where are they?" In *Storming the Tower: Women in the Academic World*. New York: Nichols/GP Publishing.

Fausto-Sterling, Anne. 1997. "Beyond Difference: A Biologist's Perspective." *Journal of Social Issues*, 53(2): 233.

Fine, Michelle, and Susan M. Gordon. 1989. "Feminist Transformations Of Psychology." In *Gender and Thought: Psychological Perspectives,* eds., Mary Crawford and Margaret Gentry. New York: Springer-Verlag.

Fine, Michelle, and Adrienne Asch. 1988. "Disability Beyond Stigma: Social Interaction, Discrimination, and Activism." *Journal of Social Issues* 44 (Spring): 3-21.

Fisher, A. B., 1992. "When Will Women Get to the Top?" *Fortune*, 126: 44-56.

Fisher, Bernice. 1998. "Wandering in the Wilderness: The Search for Women Role Models." *Signs: The Journal of Women in Culture and Society*, 12(2).

Fisher, E. 1974. "Children's Books: The Second Sex, Junior Division." In *And Jill Came Tumbling After: Sexism in American Education*, eds., J. Stacey and J. Daniels. New York: Dell.

Fiske, S. T., and Stevens, L. E. 1993. "What's So Special About Sex?: Gender Stereotyping and Discrimination." In *Gender Issues in Contemporary Society, eds.,* S. Oskamp and M. Costanzo. Newberry Park, CA: Sage Publications, Inc.

Fitzgerald, L.F. 1996. "The Prevalence of Sexual Harassment." In *Combating Sexual Harassment in Higher Education*, eds., B. Lott and M. E. Reilly. Washington, D.C.: National Education Assoc.

Flexner, S. B. and L.C. Hauck. eds. 1993. *Random House Unabridged Dictionary*, 2nd ed., New York: Random House

Florio-Ruane, Susan. 1991. "Conservation and Narrative in Collaborative Research: An Ethnography of the Written Literacy Form." In *The Private Self: Theory and Practice of Women's Autobiographical Writings*, ed., Shari Benstock. Chapel Hill: University of North Carolina Press.

Foley, Teresa, and Stephen P. Safran. 1994. "Gender-biased Language in Learning Disability Textbooks." *Journal of Learning Disabilities* 27(5): 309-14.

Form, William and Claudine Hanson. 1985. "The Consistency of Stratal Ideologies of Economic Justice." *Research in Social Stratification and Mobility,* Robert B. Robinson, ed., Vol. 4., Greenwich, CT: JAI Press.

Form, William and David B. McMillen. 1983. "Women, Men, and Machines." *Work and Occupations*, 10(2): 147-178.

Forman, Janis, ed., 1992. *New Visions of Collaborative Writing*. Portsmouth, NH: Boynton Cook.

Foster, Herbert L., and Carmen J. Iannaccone. 1994. "Multicultural Content in Special Education Introductory Textbooks." *The Journal of Special Education*, 28(1): 77-92.

Fox-Genovese, Elizabeth. 1998. "My Statue, My Self: Autobiographical Writings of Afro-American Women." In *The Private Self: Theory and Practice of Women's Autobiographical Writings*, ed., Shari Benstock. Chapel Hill: University of North Carolina Press.

Frances, C. and R. F. Mensel. 1981. "Women and Minorities in Administration of Higher Education Institutions: Employment Patterns and Salary Comparisons, A Special Report." Washington, D. C., University Personnel Association.

Franko, Patrice and Mark Boyer. 1995. "The ABC's of Case Teaching: A Manual in Progress." Paper presented at the annual meeting of the International Studies Association. Chicago, IL.

Freeman, B. C. 1977. "Faculty Women in the American University: Up the Down Staircase." *Higher Education*, 6: 165-188.

Freire, Paulo. 1970. *The Pedagogy of the Oppressed*. New York: The Continuum Publishing Company.

Friedmann, Susan Stanford. 1988. "Women's Autobiographical Selves: Theory and Practice." In *The Private Self: Theory and Practice of Women's Autobiographical Writings*, ed., Shari Benstock. Chapell Hill: University of North Carolina Press.

Gallant, M. J., and J.E. Cross. 1993. "Wayward Puritans in the Ivory Tower: Collective Aspects of Gender Discrimination in Academia." *The Sociological Quarterly*, 34(2): 237-256.

Gannon, Linda, Tracy Luchetta, Kelly Rhodes, Lynn Pardie, and Dan Segrist. 1992. "Sex Bias in Psychological Research." *American Psychologist*, 47 (March): 389-96.

Gay, Judith. 1988. "The Incidence of Photographs of Racial Minorities in Introductory Psychology Texts." *The Journal of Black Psychology,* 15 (Fall): 77-79.

Gearhart, Sally and Miller Gearhart. 1984. "Future Visions: Feminist Utopias in Review." *Women in Search of Utopia: Mavericks and Mythmakers,* eds. Ruby Rohrlich and Elaine Hoffman wazzu Baruch. New York: Schocken Press.

Geiger, Susan. 1986. "Women's Life Histories: Method and Content." *Signs*, 11: 334-351.

Germain, C. B., 1973. "An Ecological Perspective in Casework
Practice." *Social Casework*, 54: 323-330.
Gilligan, Carol. 1982. *In a Different Voice: Psychological Theory and
Women's Development.* Cambridge, MA: Harvard University Press.
Ginorio, Angela B. 1998. "Contextualizing Violence in a Participatory
Classroom: A Socially Defined Identities Approach." *Psychology of
Women Quarterly*, 22(1): 77-96.
Ginorio, Angela, and Lorraine J. Martinez. 1998. "Where Are the
Latinas? Ethno-race and Gender in Psychology Courses."
Psychology of Women Quarterly, 22(1): 53-68.
Goldstein, Susan B. 1995. "Cross-cultural Psychology as a Curriculum
Transformation Resource." *Teaching of Psychology*, 22
(December): 228-32.
Gratch, L. V., M. E. Bassett, and M. L. Attra. 1995. "The Relationship
of Gender and Ethnicity to Self-silencing and Depression Among
College Students." *Psychology of Women Quarterly*, 19: 509-16.
Greene, Beverly, and Janis Sanchez-Hucles. 1998. "Diversity:
Advancing an Inclusive Feminist Psychology.". In *Shaping the
Future of Feminist Psychology: Education, Research, and Practice,*
eds., Judith Worell and Norine Johnson. Washington, D.C.:
American Psychological Association.
Grossman, Frances K. Gilbert, Lucia A., Nancy P. Genero, Susan E.
Hawes, Janet S. Hyde, and Jeanne Marecek. 1998. "Feminist
Research: Practice and Problems." *In Shaping the Future of Feminist
Psychology: Education, Research, and Practice*, eds., Judith Worell
and Norine Johnson. Washington, D.C.: American Psychological
Association.
Gluck, Sherna, and Daphne Patai, eds., 1991. *Women's Words: The
Feminist Practice of Oral History.* New York: Routledge.
Gokhale, Anuradha A. 1995. "Collaborative Learning Enchances
Critical Thinking." *Journal of Technology Education*, 7: 4.
Goodson, Ivor, ed., 1992. *Studying Teachers' Lives.* New York:
Teachers College Press.
Gordon, Avery F. and Christopher Newfields, eds. 1996. *Mapping
Multiculturalism.* Michigan: University of Minnesota Press.
Graebner, Dianne B. 1972. "A Decade of Sexism in Readers." *The
Reading Teacher*, 25: 52-58.
Graham, Robert, J. 1991. *Reading and Writing the Self.* New York:
Teachers College Press.

Gray, Peter. 1991. *Psychology*. New York: Worth Publishers, Inc.

Grecich, David G. and Peter E. Paraschos. 1996. "Reinventing International Affairs Education: Active Learning, the Case Method, and Case Studies." Pew Case Studies in International Affairs and the Institute for the Study of Diplomacy, Georgetown University, Washington, DC.

Hall, Richard H. 1986. *Dimensions of Worth*. Beverly Hills, CA: Sage.

Hall, Roberta M., and Bernice R. Sandler. 1982. *The Classroom Climate: A Chilly One for Women?* Washington, DC: Association of American Colleges and Universities.

Haney, C., and P. G. Zimbardo. 1977. "The Socialization Into Criminality: On Becoming a Prisoner and a Guard." In *Law, Justice and the Individual in Society: Psychological and Legal Issues*, eds., J. L. Tapp, and F. L. Levine. New York: Hole, Rinehart & Winston.

Haraway, Donna. 1989. *Primate Visions: Gender, Race, and Nature in the World of Modern Science*. New York and London: Routledge.

-----1991. *Symians, Cyborgs & Women: The Reinventional Nature*. New York and London: Routledge.

Hare-Mustin, Rachel, and Jeanne Marecek. 1988. "The Meaning of Difference: Gender Theory, Postmodernism, and Psychology." *American Psychologist*, 43: 455-64.

Harste, J. 1993. "Inquiry-Based Instruction." *Primary Voices*, 2(1): 2-5.

Hawkesworth, Mary. 1989. "Knowers, Knowing, Known: Feminist Theory and Claims of Truth." *Signs*, 14(3): 533-557.

Heilbrun, Carolyn. 1988. *Writing a Women's Life*. New York: Ballantine Books.

Herndl, Diane Price. 1991. "The Dilemmas of a Feminist Dialogic." In *Feminism, Bakhtin, and the Dialogic*, eds., Dale Bauer and S. Jaret McKinstry. Albany, NY: State University Press.

Herrnstein, Richard J., and Charles Murray. 1994. *The Bell Curve: Intelligence and Class Structure in American Life*. New York: Free Press.

Higher Education Research Institute. 1993. "The American Freshman: National Norms for 1993." Los Angeles: Graduate School of Education, University of California.

Hirsch, E. D., Jr., J. F. Kett, and J. Trefil. 1991. *The Dictionary of Cultural Literacy*. Boston,MA: Houghton Mifflin Company.

Hirsch, K. 1997. "Fraternities of Fear." In *Experiencing Race, Class, and Gender in the United States,* V. Cyrus, ed. Mountain View, CA: Mayfield Publishing.

Hitchcock, M. E. and G. E. Tompkins. 1987. "Basal Readers: Are They Still Sexist?" *The Reading Teacher,* 41(3): 288-292.

Hogben, Matthew, and Caroline Waterman. 1997. "Are All of Your Students Represented in Their Textbooks? A Content Analysis of Coverage of Diversity Issues in Introductory Psychology Textbooks." *Teaching of Psychology,* 24(2): 95-100.

hooks, bell. 1981. *Ain't I a Woman: Black Women and Feminism.* Boston: South End Press.

-----1984. *Feminist Theory: From Margin to Center.* Boston: South End Press.

-----1989. *Talking Back.* Boston: South End Press.

-----1994. *Teaching to Transgress: Education as the Practice of Freedom.* New York and London: Routledge.

Hornig, L. S., 1978. "HERS Story." *Grants,* 3: 36-42.

Houston, Barbara. 1996. "Gender Freedom and the Subtleties of Sexist Education." In *The Gender Question in Education,* eds. Ann Diller, Barbara Houston, Kathryn Pauly Morgan, and Maryann Ayim. Boulder, CO: Westview.

Hughes, Kate, P. 1996. "Education for Liberation? Two Australian Contexts." In *Gender in Popular Education: Methods for Empowerment,* eds., Shirley Walters and Linzi Manicom. London and New Jersey, CACE Publications and Zed Books.

Hull, Gloria T., Patricia Bell Scott, and Barbara Smith, eds. 1982. *All the Women are White, All the Blacks are Men, But Some of Us Are Brave.* New York: The Feminist Press at the City University of New York.

Hyde, J. 1994. "Can Meta-analysis Make Feminist Transformations in Psychology?" *Psychology of Women Quarterly,* 18(4): 451-62.

Iles, Teresa, ed., 1992. *All Sides of the Subject: Women and Biography.* New York: Teachers College Press.

Irvine, J. J., and W. E. York. 1995. "Learning Styles and Culturally Diverse Students: A Literature Review." In *Handbook of Research on Multicultural Education,* eds. J. A. Banks and C. A. McGee Banks. New York: Macmillan.

Jaschok, Maria and Suzanne Miers, eds., 1994. *Women and Chinese Patriarchy.* Hong Kong and London: Hong Kong University Press and Zed Books.

Johnson, Mary A. 1997. "Implications of Multiple Intelligence Theory: Teaching Young Children Using the Project Approach." Paper presented at the Second Annual Velma E. Schmidt Conference on Early Childhood Education. University of North Texas, Denton, Texas.

Johnsrud, L. 1993. "Women and Minority Faculty Experiences: Defining and Responding to Diverse Realities." In *Building a Diverse Faculty*, eds., J. Gainen and R. Boice. San Francisco: Jossey Bass Publishers.

Jones, Terry and Gale S. Young. 1997. "Classroom Dynamics: Disclosing the Hidden Curriculum." In *Multicultural Course Transformation in Higher Education*, eds., Ann Intili Morey and Margie K. Kitano. Boston: Allyn and Bacon.

Joseph, Gloria, and Jill Lewis, eds. 1981. *Common Differences: Conflicts in Black and White Feminist Perspectives*. New York: Anchor/Doubleday.

Jordan, Glenn and Chris Weedon. 1995. *Cultural Politics: Class, Gender, Race and the Postmodern World*. Cambridge, MA: Basil Blackwell.

Kahn, Arnold S., and Janice D. Yoder. 1989. "The Psychology of Women and Conservatism: Rediscovering Social Change." *Psychology of Women Quarterly*, 13:417-32.

Kamin, Leon J. 1974. *The Science and Politics of IQ*. Potomac, MD: Lawrence Erlbaum.

Katz, Daniel and Robert L. Kahn. 1978. *The Social Psychology of Organizations*. 2nd ed., New York: Wiley.

Keller, Evelyn Fox. 1985. *Reflections on Gender and Science*. New Haven, CT: Yale University Press.

Kelly, George. 1963. *A Theory of Personality: The Psychology of Personal Constructs*. New York: W. W. Norton.

Kimmel, Ellen, and Judith Worell. 1998. "Preaching What We Practice: Principles and Strategies in Feminist Pedagogy." In *Shaping the Future of Feminist Psychology: Education, Research, and Practice*, eds., Judith Worell and Norine Johnson. Washington, D.C.: American Psychological Association.

Kitano, Margie K. 1997. "A Rationale and Framework for Course Change." *Multicultural Course Transformation in Higher Education*, eds. , Ann Intili Morey and Margie K. Kitano. Boston: Allyn and Bacon.

Kitano, Margie. 1997. "What a Course Will Look Like After
Multicultural Change." In *Multicultural Course Transformation in Higher Education*, eds., Ann Intili Morey and Margie K. Kitano. Boston: Allyn and Bacon.

Knopp, L., 1996. "Women in Higher Education Today: A Mid-1990s Profile." *Research Briefs*, 6: 1-11.

Knowles, J. Gary. 1992. "Models for Understanding Pre-Service and Beginning Teachers' Biographies: Illustrations from Case Studies." In *Studying Teachers' Lives*, ed., Ivor Goodson. New York: Teachers College Press.

Kohn, Melvin L. 1990. *Social Structure and Self-Direction.* Cambridge, MA: Basil Blackwell.

Korn/Ferry International and UCLA Anderson Graduate School of Management. 1992. "Decade of the Executive Woman." One in a series of studies coordinated by Southern California Search Practice, 1-57.

Koss, Mary P., L. A. Goodman, A. Browne, Louise Fitzgerald, Gwendolyn P. Keita, and Nancy Felipe Russo. 1994. *No Safe Haven: Male Violence Against Women at Home, at Work, and in the Community.* Washington, D.C.: American Psychological Association.

Koss, Mary P., and M. R. Harvey. 1994. "Rape is Widespread." In *Violence Against Women*, B. Leone, ed., San Diego, CA: Greenhaven Press

Kuhn, Thomas. 1962. *The Structure of Scientific Revolutions.* Chicago: University of Chicago Press.

Lakoff, Robin. 1973. "Language and Women's Place." *Language and Society*, 2:45-79.

Landrine, Hope, ed. 1995. *Bringing Cultural Diversity to Feminist Psychology.* Washington, D.C.: American Psychological Association.

Landrine, Hope, Elizabeth A. Klonoff, and A. Brown-Collins. 1995. "Cultural Diversity and Methodology in Feminist Psychology: Critique, Proposal, Empirical Example." In *Bringing Cultural Diversity to Feminist Psychology*, ed., Hope Landrine. Washington, D.C.: American Psychological Association.

Lather, Patti. 1986. "Research as Praxis." *Harvard Educational Review*, 56: 257-277.

Lee, V. E., C. Lewis-Mackie, and H.M. Marks. 1993. "Persistence to the Baccalaureate Degree for Students Who Transfer From Community College." *American Journal of Education*, 102: 80-114.

Lester, Nancy, John Mayher, Cindy Onore, and Gordan Pradl. 1983. *Learning to Write/Writing To Learn*. Upper Monclair, NJ.

Lever, J. 1978. "Sex Differences in the Complexity of Children's Play and Games." *American Sociological Review*, 43: 471-483.

Levin, H. 1993. "Learning From Accelerated Schools." In *Selecting and Integrating School Improvement Programs*, eds., J.H. Block, S. T. Everson, and T. R. Guskey. New York: Scholastic Books.

Lewin, Miriam, and Cheryl L. Wild. 1991. "The Impact of the Feminist Critique on Tests, Assessment and Methodology." *Psychology of Women Quarterly*, 15(4): 581-96.

Lewis, M. 1991. "Gender Equity: The State of Play in Early Childhood Services." Paper Presented at the Early Childhood Convention. Dunedin, New Zealand, September 8-12.

Lewis, Rena B. 1997. "Assessment of Student Learning," In *Multicultural Course Transformation in Higher Education*, eds., Ann Intili Morey and Margie K. Kitano. Boston: Allyn and Bacon.

Lie, S. L. and V. O'Leary. 1990. *Storming the Tower: Women in the Academic World*. New York: Nichols/GP Publishing.

Lin, Y, and W. P. Vogt. 1996. "Occupational Outcomes for Students Earning Two-Year College Degrees. *Journal of Higher Education*, 67(4): 446-475.

Lincoln, Yvonne, and Egon Guba. 1985. *Naturalistic Inquiry*. Beverley Hills: Sage Publications.

Lloyd, B., and C. Smith. 1985. "The Social Representation of Gender and Young Children's Play." *British Journal of Developmental Psychology*, 3: 65-73.

Lott, Albert. 1988. "Cultural Diversity in the Undergraduate Social Psychology Course." In *Teaching a Psychology of People: Resources for Gender and Sociocultural Awareness*, eds., Phyllis Bronstein and Kathryn Quina. Washington, D.C.: American Psychological Association.

Lynch, Eleanor. 1997. "Instructional Strategies." *Multicultural Course Transformation in Higher Education*, eds., Ann Intili Morey and Margie K. Kitano. Boston: Allyn and Bacon.

Maccoby, E. E. and C. M. Jacklin. 1974. *The Psychology of Sex Differences*. Stanford, CA:Stanford University Press.

Madden, Margaret E., and Janet Shibley Hyde. 1998. "Integrating
    Gender and Ethnicity Into Psychology Courses. " *Psychology of
    Women Quarterly, 22*: 1-12.
------, Eds. 1998. "Integrating Gender and Ethnicity Into Psychology
    Courses." *Psychology of Women Quarterly*, 22. [Special Issue].
Madden, Margaret E., and Nancy Felipe Russo. 1997. *Women in the
    Curriculum: Psychology*. Towson, MD: National Center for
    Curriculum Transformation Resources for Women.
Marecek, Jeanne. 1993. "Disappearance, Silences, and Anxious
    Rhetoric: Gender in Abnormal Psychology Textbooks." *Journal of
    Theoretical and Philosophical Psychology*, 13(2): 114-23.
------. 1995. "Gender, Politics, and Psychology's Ways of Knowing."
    American Psychologist, 50: 162-63.
Marshall, S. P., and C. Hatcher. 1996. "Promoting Career
    Development Through CADRE." *Educational Leadership*,
    53(6): 42-49.
Martell, R. F. 1996. "What Mediates Gender Bias in Work Behavior
    Settings?" *Sex Roles*, 35: 153-169.
Martin, B. Jr., and J. Archambault. 1986. *White Dynamite and the
    Curly Kidd*. New York: Henry Holt.
Maslow, Abraham H. 1954. *Motivation and Personality*. New York:
    Harper and Brothers.
Mayer, John. 1990. *Uncommon Sense: Theoretical Practice in
    Language Education*. Portsmouth, NH: Boynton-Cook.
McDermott, J. F. Jr., T. Wen-Shing and T. W. Maretzki, eds., 1980.
    People and Cultures of Hawaii: A Psychocultural Profile.
    Honolulu, HI: John A. Burns School of Medicine and University
    of Hawaii Press.
McIntosh, Peggy. 1983. *Interactive Phases of Curricular Re-vision*.
    (Working Paper No. 124). Wellesley, MA: Wellesley College,
    Center for Research on Women.
------. 1993. "White Privilege and Male Privilege: A Personal Account
    of Coming to See Correspondences Through Work in Women's
    Studies." In *Gender Basics*, Ed. A. Minas. Belmont, CA:
    Wadsworth Press.
McIntosh, Peggy. 1989. "Curricular Re-vision: The New Knowledge
    for a New Age." In *Educating the Majority: Women Challenge
    Tradition in Higher Education*, eds. , Carol S. Pearson, D. L.
    Shavlikl, and Judith G. Touchton. New York: Collier-Macmillan.

McKeachie, William J. 1986. *Teaching Tips: A Guidebook for the Beginning College Teacher (8th Edition)*. Lexington, MA: D.C. Heath.

McWhirter, E. H. 1997. "Perceived Barriers to Education and Career: Ethnic and Gender Differences." *Journal of Vocational Behavior*, 50(1): 124-140.

Mednick, Martha T., and Laura T. Urbanski. 1991. "The Origins and Activities of APA's Division of the Psychology of Women." *Psychology of Women Quarterly*, 15(4): 651-64.

Mernissi, Fatima. 1987. *Beyond the Veil: Male-Female Dynamics in a Modern Muslim Society*. Bloomington: Indiana University Press.

Middleton, Sue. 1992. "Developing a Radical Pedagogy: Autobiography of a New Zealand Sociologist of Women's Education." In *Studying Teacher's Lives*, ed., Ivor Goodson. New York: Teachers College Press.

Milgram, Stanley. 1974. *Obedience to Authority: An Experimental View*. New York: Harper & Row.

Miller, Kenneth L. and Susan M. Miller. 1997. *Survey of Cultural Attitudes and Behaviors*. (On-line). (CD-Rom). Abstract from: CDP. File: HaPI-CD. HaPI Items: 3038.

Miller, L. 1997. "Not Just Weapons of the Weak: Gender Harassment as a form of protest for Army Men." *Social Psychology Quarterly*, 60(1): 32-51.

Miller, Nancy. 1991. Getting Personal: Feminist Occasions and Other Autobiographical Acts. New York: Routledge.

Miller, Susan M. , Kenneth L. Miller, and L.K. Gwaltney. 1998. "Teacher Educators' Cultural Attitudes and Behaviors: Texas Survey Results." *Teacher Education and Practice*, 14(1): 30-42.

Miller, Susan M., Kenneth L. Miller, and Gwen Schroth. 1997. "Is Higher Education Free From Bias: Perceptions of Graduates From Teacher Education Programs." Proceedings of the 10th Annual Conference: Women in Higher Education, USA, 292-99.

-----1997. "Teacher Perceptions of Multicultural Training in Preservice Programs." *Journal of Instructional Psychology*, 24(4): 222-232.

Minnich, Elizabeth K. 1989. "From the Circle of the Elite to the World of the Whole: Education Equality and Excellence." In *Educating the Majority: Women Challenge Tradition in Higher Education*, eds., Pearson, Shavlik, and Touchton. New York: Collier-Macmillan.

Mohanty, Chandra, et al., eds., 1991. *Third World Women and the Politics of Feminism*. Bloomington and Indianapolis: Indiana University Press.

Monk, Janice, Anne Betteridge and Amy Newhall. 1991. "Introduction: Reaching for Global Feminism in the Curriculum." *Women's Studies International Forum*, 14(4): 277-283.

Moore, Melanie, and Richard Trahan. 1997. "Biased and Political: Student Perceptions of Females Teaching About Gender." *College Student Journal*, 31(4): 434-44.

Morey, A. I. and M. Kitano, eds. 1997. *Multicultural Course Transformation in Higher Education*. Boston: Allyn and Bacon.

Moses, Y. 1989. *Black Women in Academe: Issues and Strategies*. Association of American Colleges, US Department of Education.

Moyer, R. S. 1997. "Covering Gender on Memory's Front Page: Men's Prominence and Women's Prospects." *Sex Roles*, 37(7/8): 595-618.

Naff, K.C. 1995. "Subjective versus Objective Discrimination in Government: Adding to the Picture of Barriers to the Advancement of Women. *Political Research Quarterly*, 48: 535-555.

National Center for Education Statistics. 1992. *Students at less than 4 year institutions*, (Statistical Analysis Report NCES 92-206). Washington, DC: US Government Printing Office.

National Center for Education Statistics. 1994. *Digest of Education Statistics*, (Report NCES 94-115). Washington, DC: US Government Printing Office.

Nieto, S. 1992. *Affirming Diversity: The Sociopolitical Context of Multicultural Education*. NY: Longman.

Nolte Lensink, Judy. 1991. "Strategies for Integrating International Material into the Introductory Women's Studies Course." *Women's Studies International Forum*, 14(4): 277-283.

Norrell, J. E. and T.H. Norrell. 1996. "Faculty and Family Policies in Higher Education." *Journal of Family Issues*, 17(2): 204-226.

O'Connell, Agnes N., and Nancy F. Russo, eds., 1990. *Women in Psychology: A Bibliographic Sourcebook*. NY: Greenwood Press.

------. eds., 1991. "Women's Heritage m Psychology, Origins, Development, and Future Directions." *Psychology of Women Quarterly*, 15 [Special Issue].

O'Leary, V. and J. Mitchell. 1990. "Women Connecting With Women: Networks and Mentors in the US." In *Storming the Tower: Women in the Academic World*. New York: Nichols/GP Publishing.

Okazaki, Sumi. 1998. "Teaching Gender Issues in Asian American Psychology: A Pedagogical Framework." *Psychology of Women Quarterly,* 22(1): 33-52.

Olsen, D., S. Maple, and F. Stage. 1991. "Women and Minority Faculty Job Satisfaction: A Structural Model Examining the Effects of Professional Role Interests, Professional Satisfaction, and Institutional Fit." Paper presented to the Association for the Study of Higher Education, Boston, Massachusetts.

Oskamp, S. and M. Constanzo. 1993. "An Introduction to Gender Issues." In *Gender Issues in Contemporary Society,* S. Oskamp and M. Costanzo, eds., Newberry Park, CA: Sage.

Ottinger, C. and R. Sikula. 1993. "Women in Higher Education: Where Do We Stand?" *Research Briefs,* 4: 1-12.

Owen, C.L. and W. D. Todor. 1993. "Attitudes Toward Women as Managers: Still the Same." *Business Horizons,* 36: 12-16.

Pagano, Jo Anne. 1994. "Teaching Women." In *The Education Feminism Reader,* ed., Lynda Stone. New York and London: Routledge.

Paley, V., 1984. *Boys and Girls.* Chicago: University of Chicago.

Park., S. 1994. "Am I Qualified? Gender Bias in University Tenure and Promotion Criteria." Paper presentation, January 7, International Women in Higher Education, Orlando, Florida.

Pascarella, E. T., E. J. Whitt, M. I. Edison, A. Nora, L. S. Hagedorn, P. M. Yeager, and P.T. Terenzini. 1997. "Women's Perceptions of a 'Chilly Climate' and Their Cognitive Outcomes During the First Year of College." *Journal of College Student Development,* 38(2): 109-124.

Pearson, Carol S., Donna L. Shavlik, and Judith G. Touchton, eds., 1989. *Educating the Majority: Women Challenge Tradition in Higher Education.* New York: Collier Macmillan.

Perry, D. G., A. J. White, and Louise C. Perry. "Does Early Sex Typing Result From Children's Attempts to Match Their Behavior to Sex Role Stereotypes?" *Child Development,* 55(6): 2114-2121.

Perry, W. G. 1981. "Cognitive and Ethical Growth: The Making of Meaning." ed., A. Chickering. In *The Modern American College.* San Francisco: Jossey-Bass.

Perry, William. 1969. *Forms of Intellectual and Ethical Development in the College Years.* New York: Holt.

Peterson, Sharyl Bender, and Traci Kroner. 1992. "Gender Biases in Textbooks for Introductory Psychology and Human Development. " *Psychology of Women Quarterly*, 16: 1736.

Peterson, V. Spike and Anne Sisson Runyon. 1993. *Global Gender Issues*. Boulder, CO: Westview Press.

Pettman, Jan Jindy. 1996. *Worlding Women: A Feminist International Politics*. Sydney: Allen and Unwin.

Phillip, M. C., 1993. "Tenure Trap: Number of Obstacles Stand in Way of Tenure for Women." *Black Issues in Higher Education*, 19(17): 42-44.

Progogine, I., and Stengers. 1984. *Order Out of Chaos*. NY: Bantam Books.

Quay, L. C., D. A. Minore, and L. M. Frazier. 1993. "Sex Typing in Stories and Comprehension, Recall, and Sex-Typed Beliefs in Preschool Children." Paper Presented at the Biennial Meeting of the Society for Research in Child Development. New Orleans, LA.

Quina, K., and J. Kulberg. 1988. "The Experimental Psychology Course." In *Teaching a Psychology of People: Resources for Gender and Sociocultural Awareness*, eds., P. Bronstein and K. Quina. Washington, D.C.: American Psychological Association.

Ranson, M. R. 1990. "Gender Segregation by Field in Higher Education." *Research in Higher Education*, 31(5): 477-491.

Reid, P. T. 1990. "African American Women in Academia: Paradoxes and Barriers." In *Storming the Tower: Women in the Academic World*, eds., S. L. Lie and V. O'Leary. New York: Nichols/GP Publishing.

Reid, Pamela Trotman. 1993. "Poor Women in Psychological Research: Shut up and Shut Out." *Psychology of Women Quarterly* 17(2): 133-50.

Reid, Pamela Trotman, and Elizabeth Kelly. 1994. "Research on Women of Color: From Ignorance to Awareness." *Psychology of Women Quarterly*, 18(4): 477-86.

Reinharz, Shulamit. 1992. Feminist Methods in Social Research. New York: Oxford University Press.

Report of the Majority Staff of the Senate Judiciary Committee. May 1993. *The Response to Rape: Detours on the Road to Equal Justice*. Washington, DC.

Riger, S. and P. Galligan. 1980. "Women in Management: An Exploration of Competing Paradigms." *American Psychologist*, 35(10): 902-910.

Rohrbaugh, J. B. 1979. *Women: Psychology's Puzzle*. NY: Basic Books.

Rosenfelt, Deborah S. 1997. "Doing Multiculturalism: Conceptualizing Curricular Change." In *Multicultural Course Transformation in Higher Education*, eds., Ann Intili Morey and Margie K. Kitano. Boston: Allyn and Bacon.

Rosinsky, Natalie M. 1982. *Feminist Futures: Contemporary Women's Speculative Fiction*. Ann Arbor: UMI Research.

Rosser, Sue V. 1990. *Female-friendly Science: Applying Women's Studies Methods and Theories to Attract Students*. Elmsford, NY: Pergamon.

Roy, Anna. 1993. "Unlearning Heterosexual Bias in the Classroom." *Psychology of Women: Newsletter of Division 35. American Psychological Association,* 20 (Winter): 6.

Ruble, D. N. and T.L.Ruble. 1982. 'Sex Stereotypes." In *In the Eye Of the Beholder: Contemporary Issues in Stereotyping*, ed., A. G. Miller. New York: Praeger.

Russ, Joanna. 1981. "Recent Feminist Utopias." In *Future Females: A Critical Anthology,* ed., Marleen S. Barr. Bowling Green State University Popular Press.

Sadker, M. and David Sadker. 1982. *Sex Equity Handbook for Schools*. New York: Longman.

-----1986. "Sexism in the Classroom: From Grade School to Graduate School." *Phi Delta Kappan*, 67(7): 512-515.

-----1994. *Failing at Fairness: How Schools Cheat Our Girls*. NY: Touchton.

Sadker, M., D. Sadker, and L. Long. 1989. "Gender and Educational Equality." In *Multicultural Education: Issues and Perspectives*, eds., J. A. Banks and C. A. Banks. Boston: Allyn & Bacon.

Sandler, Bernice. 1993. "Women as Mentors: Myths and Commandments." The Chronicle Of Higher Education. March 10.

Sandler, Bernice, Lisa Silverberg, and Roberta Hall. 1996. *The Chilly Classroom Climate, A Guide to Improve the Education of Women*. Washington, DC: National Association for Women in Education.

Santos de Barona, Maryann, and Pamela Trotman Reid. 1992. "Ethnic Issues in Teaching the Psychology of Women." *Teaching of Psychology,* 19(2): 96-99.

Sarkees, Meredith Reid and Nancy McGlen. 1995. "Backlash Toward Studying the Status of Women in Political Science and International Studies." Paper presented at the annual meeting of the International Studies Association. Chicago, IL.

Sax, L. J., A. W. Astin, M. Arredondo, and W.S. Korn. 1996. *The American College Teacher: National Norms for the 1995-96 HERI Faculty Survey.* Los Angeles, CA: Higher Education Research Institute, UCLA.

Schiebinger, Londa. 1993. *Nature's Body: Gender in the Making of Modern Science.* Boston: Beacon Press.

Schroth, Gwen, Kenneth L. Miller, and Susan M. Miller. 1997. "Principals' Perceptions of Multicultural Training in Their Mid-Management Programs." Paper presented at the National Council of Professors in Educational Administration, Vail, CO.

Schroth, Gwen, Susan L. Miller, Kenneth L. Miller. 1998. "Educators' Perceptions of Multicultural Training in Their Preparation Programs." Paper presented at the annual meeting of the American Educational Research Association, San Diego, CA.

Scott, K. P. 1986. "Effects of Sex-Fair Reading Material on Pupil's Attitudes, Comprehension, And Interest." *American Educational Research Journal*, 23: 105-116.

Seals, B. 1997. "Faculty-to-Faculty Sexual Harassment." In *Sexual Harassment on Campus*, eds., B. R. Sandler and R. J. Shoop. Needham Heights, MA: Allyn & Bacon.

Shakeshaft, Carol. 1986. "A Gender Risk." *Phi Delta Kappan.* March: 499-503.

Shapiro, L., 1990. "Guns and Dolls." *Newsweek*, 28 May, 54-65.

Shields, Stephanie A. 1975. "Functionalism, Darwinism, and the Psychology of Women: A Study in Social Myth." *American Psychologist*, 30: 379-754.

Simoni, Jane M. 1996. "Confronting Heterosexism in the Teaching of Psychology." *Teaching of Psychology*, 23(4): 220-26.

Smith, Barbara. 1983. *Home Girls: A Black Feminist Anthology.* New York: Kitchen Table: Women of Color Press.

Solomon, B. M. 1985. *In the Companu of Educated Women: A History of Women and Higher Education in America.* New Haven, CT: Yale University Press.

Southern Poverty Law Center. 1997. "Anti-homosexual Crime: The Severity of the Violence Shows the Hatred." *Intelligence Report*, 88: 16-17.

Spence, J. 1993. "Women, Men, and Society: Plus Ca Change, Plus C'est La Meme Chose." In *Gender Issues in Contemporary Society*, eds., S. Oskamp and M. Costanzo. Newberry Park, CA: Sage.

Sprock, J. and C. Y. Yoder. 1997. "Women and Depression: An Update on the Report of the APA Task Force." *Sex Roles*, 35 (5/6): 269-303.

Stanford, B. H. 1992. "Gender Equity in the Classroom." In *Common Bonds: Anti-Bias Teaching in a Diverse Society*, eds., D. A. Byrnes and G. Kiger. Wheaton, MD: Association of Childhood Education International.

Stanworth, Michelle. 1981. *Gender and Schooling: A Study of Sexual Divisions in the Classroom*. London: Unwin-Hyman.

Stepnick, A. and J.D. Orcutt. 1996. "Conflicting Testimony: Judges' and Attorneys' Perceptions of Gender Bias in Legal Settings." *Sex Roles*, 34(7/8): 567-579.

Sterling, T. D., W. L. Rosenbaum, and J. J. Weinkam. 1995. "Publication Decisions Revisited: The Effect of the Outcome of Statistical Tests on the Decision to Publish and Vice Versa." *American Statistician,* 49: 108-12.

Sue, D. W. and D. Sue. 1990. *Counseling the Culturally Different: Theory and Practice*. 2nd ed., New York: John Wiley and Sons.

Task Force on Representation in the Curriculum. 1995. "Including Diverse Women in the Undergraduate Curriculum.": #ED 406 632 CG027631. ERIC/CASS. Task Force on *Resources in Education* Representation in the Curriculum of the Division of Psychology of Women of the American Psychological Association.

Taylor, A. J. P. 1975. *The Second World War*. New York: Putnam.

Tiefer, Lenore. 1991. "A Brief History of the Association for Women in Psychology: 1969-1991. " Psychology of Women Quarterly, 15(4): 635-50.

Touchton, J. and L. Davis. 1991. *Fact Book on Women in Higher Education*. New York: American Council on Education, Macmillan Publishers.

Torgovnick, Marianna. 1991. *Gone Primitive: Savage Intellects, Modern Lives*. Chicago: University of Chicago Press.

-----1997. *Primitive Passions: Men, Women, and the Quest for Ecstasy*. New York: Alfred A. Knopf.

Traver, Bob. 1987. "Autobiography, Feminism, and the Study of Teaching." New York: A. Knopf.

Traver, Bob. 1987. "Autobiography, Feminism, and the Study of Teaching." *Harvard Educational Review*, 88: 443-45.

Truax, A. T. 1996. "Sexual Harassment in Higher Education: What We've Learned." In *Combatting Sexual Harassment in Higher Education*, eds., B. Lott and M.E. Reilly. Washington, DC: National Education Association.

Valentine, S. and G. Mosley. 1998. "Aversion to Women Who Work and Perceived Discrimination Among Euro-Americans and Mexican-Americans." *Perceptual and Motor Skills*, 86(3): 1027-33.

Verrier, D. 1992. "On Becoming Tenured: Acquiring Academic Tenure at a Research University." Paper presented at the Association for Higher Education.

Wallace, J. M. 1986. "Nurturing an 'I Can' Attitude in Mathematics." *Equity and Choice*, 2(2): 35-40.

Walker, Lenore. 1979. *The Battered Woman*. NY: Harper & Row.

Weber, Lynn. 1998. "A Conceptual Framework for Understanding Race, Class, Gender, and Sexuality." *Psychology of Women Quarterly*, 22(1): 13-32.

Weiler, Kathleen. 1988. *Women Teaching for Change: Gender, Class, and Power*. New York: Bergin & Garvey.

Welch., L. 1990. Women in Higher Education: Changes and *Challenges*. New York: Praeger.

Wells, J. W. and A. Daly. 1992. "University Students' Felt Alienation and Their Attitudes Toward African-Americans, Women and Homosexuals." *Psychological Reports*, 70: 623-26.

Wilson, Midge and Kathy Russell. 1996. *Divided Sisters: Bridging the Gap Between Black Women and White Women*. New York: Anchor-Doubleday.

Witherell, Carol, and Nel Noddings, eds., 1991. *Stories Lives Tell: Narrative and Dialogue in Education*. NY: Teachers College Press.

Women in Higher Education. 4.2, (Feb. 1995): 1.

Worell, Judith, and Norine G. Johnson, eds., 1997. *Shaping the Future of Feminist Psychology: Education, Research, and Practice*. Washington, D.C.: American Psychological Association.

Worell, Judith, and Damon Robinson. 1994. "Reinventing Analogue Methods for Research with Women." *Psychology of Women Quarterly*, 18(4): 463-76.

Worell, Judith, and Claire Etaugh. 1994. "Transforming Theory and Research with Women: Themes and Variations." *Psychology of Women Quarterly* 18: 443-50.

Wright., C. and S. Wright. 1987. "The Role of Mentors in the Career Development of Young Professionals." *Family Relations*, 36: 204-8.

Wyche, Karen Fraser. 1998. "Teaching the Psychology of Women Courses in Another Discipline: The Case of African American Studies." *Psychology of Women Quarterly*, 22(1): 69-76.

Wyche, Karen Fraser, and Joy K. Rice. 1998. "Feminist Therapy: From Dialogue to Tenets." In *Shaping the Future of Feminist Psychology: Education, Research, and Practice*, eds., Judith Worell and Norine Johnson. Washington, D.C.: American Psychological Association.

Index